Pricing Strategy Implen

Pricing can truly transform organizations. The impact of pricing on organizations is a result of two factors: pricing strategy development and the implementation of these strategies. Implementation is arguably the most difficult part in the pricing strategy process where even seasoned practitioners demand guidance. Pricing strategy development requires creativity, analytical rigor, and an ability to master the internal political competition for scarce resources, but it takes place in a well-defined environment. Fast forward to strategy implementation: competitors that stubbornly fail to behave according to assumptions, new entrants, internal resistance, new opportunities, changing customer preferences, leadership changes, regulatory interventions, or market growth rates that change unexpectedly are some of the intervening variables between the pricing strategy originally developed and the strategy actually implemented. This book provides the theories and best practices that enable the effective implementation of pricing strategies. It offers:

- a best practice overview on how to convert a pricing strategy into superior results
- insights from current academic research on driving profits via pricing strategy implementation
- examples on how to deal with digital transformation in the context of pricing
- tools and insights into how to overcome internal resistance, align the organization, and forge win-win relationships with customers

Taking a new approach, *Pricing Strategy Implementation* is a critical and practical tool for practicing executives and managers, as well as academics and researchers in pricing, marketing strategy, and strategic management.

Andreas Hinterhuber is an Associate Professor at the Department of Management at Università Ca' Foscari Venezia, Italy, and has been a Partner of Hinterhuber & Partners, a consulting company specializing in pricing based in Innsbruck, Austria. He has published articles in leading journals including *Journal of Business Research* and *MIT Sloan Management Review*, and has edited many books on pricing, including *Innovation in Pricing* (2012), *The ROI of Pricing* (2014), *Pricing and the Sales Force* (2015), and *Value First then Price* (2017).

Stephan M. Liozu is Chief Value Officer of the Thales Group (www.thalesgroup.com); the founder of Value Innoruption Advisors (www.valueinnoruption.com) – a consulting boutique specializing in value-based pricing, data monetization, and digital pricing – and he is an Adjunct Professor and Research Fellow at the Weatherhead School of Management at Case Western Reserve University, USA. Stephan sits on the Advisory Board of LeveragePoint Innovation and of the Professional Pricing Society. He is the author of multiple books about pricing, including *Pricing and Human Capital* (2015), and co-editor of *Innovation in Pricing* (2012), *The ROI of Pricing* (2014), and *Pricing and the Sales Force* (2015).

Pricing Strategy Implementation
Translating Pricing Strategy into Results

Andreas Hinterhuber and Stephan M. Liozu

LONDON AND NEW YORK

First published 2020
by Routledge
2 Park Square, Milton Park, Abingdon, Oxon OX14 4RN

and by Routledge
52 Vanderbilt Avenue, New York, NY 10017

Routledge is an imprint of the Taylor & Francis Group, an informa business

© 2020 Andreas Hinterhuber and Stephan M. Liozu

The right of Andreas Hinterhuber and Stephan M. Liozu to be identified as the authors of the editorial material, and of the authors for their individual chapters, has been asserted in accordance with sections 77 and 78 of the Copyright, Designs and Patents Act 1988.

All rights reserved. No part of this book may be reprinted or reproduced or utilised in any form or by any electronic, mechanical, or other means, now known or hereafter invented, including photocopying and recording, or in any information storage or retrieval system, without permission in writing from the publishers.

Trademark notice: Product or corporate names may be trademarks or registered trademarks, and are used only for identification and explanation without intent to infringe.

British Library Cataloguing-in-Publication Data
A catalogue record for this book is available from the British Library

Library of Congress Cataloging-in-Publication Data
Names: Hinterhuber, Andreas, editor. | Liozu, Stephan, editor.
Title: Pricing strategy implementation: translating pricing strategy into results/ [edited by] Andreas Hinterhuber and Stephan M. Liozu.
Description: Abingdon, Oxon; New York, NY: Routledge, 2020. |
Includes bibliographical references and index. |
Identifiers: LCCN 2019016050 (print) | LCCN 2019018059 (ebook) |
ISBN 9780429446849 (E-Book) | ISBN 9781138332164 (hardback) |
ISBN 9781138332171 (pbk.)
Subjects: LCSH: Pricing.
Classification: LCC HF5416.5 (ebook) | LCC HF5416.5 .P743 2020 (print) |
DDC 658.8/16—dc23
LC record available at https://lccn.loc.gov/2019016050

ISBN: 978-1-138-33216-4 (hbk)
ISBN: 978-1-138-33217-1 (pbk)
ISBN: 978-0-429-44684-9 (ebk)

Typeset in Bembo
by Deanta Global Publishing Services, Chennai, India

Contents

List of contributors   vii

PART 1
Introduction   1

1   Introduction: Implementing pricing strategies   3
     ANDREAS HINTERHUBER AND STEPHAN M. LIOZU

PART 2
Aligning the organization around pricing strategy implementation   9

2   Implementing pricing strategies: The frameworks to drive profits by pricing actions   11
     ANDREAS HINTERHUBER

3   Elevating the cost of doing nothing: An interview with Mark Shafer   22
     ANDREAS HINTERHUBER, EVANDRO POLLONO, AND MARK SHAFER

PART 3
Pricing strategy implementation: The role of the sales force   35

4   The role of the sales force in pricing strategy implementation   37
     ANDREAS HINTERHUBER AND FRANK CESPEDES

5   The strategic account manager as ecosystem captain: Driving profits via pricing   45
     ANDREAS HINTERHUBER AND BERNARD QUANCARD

6   Designing sales force compensation programs to improve pricing execution   55
     STEPHAN M. LIOZU

PART 4
Pricing strategy implementation: The role of marketing 69

7 Implementing pricing strategy by developing and
implementing effective discounting practices 71
EVANDRO POLLONO AND JOSE VELA

8 Designing and executing B2B customer segmentation 78
STEPHAN M. LIOZU AND KATIE RICHARDSON

9 Training programs to boost pricing execution 87
STEPHAN M. LIOZU

10 Implementing a structured pricing strategy approach 92
INGO HENNECKE

PART 5
Implementing pricing strategies that win deals 101

11 Pricing large deals: Insights into capabilities and tools that help
to win large deals profitably 103
ANDREAS HINTERHUBER

12 Pricing to win: A framework for strategic bid decision-making 111
GERHARD RIEHL

13 Value quantification: Processes and best practices to document and
quantify value in B2B 122
ANDREAS HINTERHUBER

14 Implementing pricing strategies via quantified value propositions 136
TODD SNELGROVE

15 Adopt value selling: Best practices to drive sustainable
organizational change 142
PEYTON MARSHALL

16 Executing price control in five simple steps 151
MITCHELL D. LEE

17 Eight best practices to improve pricing execution 159
STEPHAN M. LIOZU

Index 163

Contributors

Frank Cespedes is Senior Lecturer in the Entrepreneurial Management Unit at Harvard Business School, Boston, MA, where he has developed and taught a variety of MBA and executive courses, led the Strategic Marketing Management program for senior executives, and was co-lead of the Sustainable Market Leadership program for CEOs and their leadership teams. Before joining the faculty, he was a Research Associate at Harvard and worked at Bain & Company.

Ingo Hennecke is the Global Pricing Manager of Crop Science, Bayer AG Leverkusen, Germany, and leads the pricing strategy and value pricing activities. Prior to his current position, he was responsible for global customer management initiatives, heading the operational business in Austria, and managing some of the company's major brands. With more than 25 years of experience in managerial positions, Hennecke is a highly recognized in-house consultant for sales and marketing organizations, and a regular speaker at international conferences.

Andreas Hinterhuber is an Associate Professor at the Department of Management at Università Ca' Foscari Venezia, Italy, and has been a Partner of Hinterhuber & Partners, a consulting company specializing in pricing based in Innsbruck, Austria. He has published articles in leading journals including *Journal of Business Research* and *MIT Sloan Management Review* and has edited many books on pricing, including *Innovation in Pricing* (2012), *The ROI of Pricing* (2014), *Pricing and the Sales Force* (2016), and *Value First then Price* (2017).

Mitchell D. Lee is Profit Evangelist for the intelligent-pricing, margin-optimization, and commercial-excellence solutions provider Vendavo. He has over 25 years of experience in the technical, operational, marketing, and commercial arenas of the chemical industry. Prior to Vendavo, Lee was with BASF and Orica in product marketing and business management, driving operational optimization, pricing excellence, and margin improvement.

Stephan M. Liozu is Chief Value Officer of the Thales Group (www.thalesgroup.com); the founder of Value Innoruption Advisors (www.valueinnoruption.com) – a consulting boutique specializing in value-based pricing, data monetization, and digital pricing; and he is an Adjunct Professor and Research Fellow at the Weatherhead School of Management at Case Western Reserve University, Cleveland, OH. Liozu sits on the advisory boards of LeveragePoint Innovation and the Professional Pricing Society. He is the author of multiple books about pricing, including *Pricing and Human Capital* (2015), and co-editor of *Innovation in Pricing* (2012), *The ROI of Pricing* (2014), and *Pricing and the Sales Force* (2015).

Peyton Marshall is the CEO of LeveragePoint Innovations, a software company providing a cloud platform for B2B enterprises implementing value strategies and value selling. Previously, he served in product management, sales, and senior management roles in a number of B2B sectors. He has also been an investment banker at Goldman Sachs and other financial services firms, structuring and selling complex financial solutions to global corporate and financial institution CFOs.

Evandro Pollono is a Managing Director of Hinterhuber & Partners, based in Milan, Italy, where he is responsible for operations in Italy, and he is a visiting lecturer on strategic pricing at the University of Alcala de Henares in Spain. He has successfully completed numerous B2C and B2B pricing projects for many leading international companies including Exxelia, Lufthansa AirPlus, Fazer, Fercam, Swarco, Tieto, Bosch, and VPS.

Bernard Quancard has been President and CEO of the Strategic Account Management Association since 2006. He has previously worked for The Boston Consulting Group; Telemecanique (Schneider Electric Group); and Schneider Global Business Development (SGBD), the entity managing global strategic accounts (GSAs) for Schneider Electric worldwide.

Katie Richardson is responsible for industry, market, competitive, and comparable research for CGI's Global Emerging Technology Practice. With 20-plus years in the manufacturing sector, Richardson's roles have spanned the Industrial Internet of Things (IIoT), Industry 4.0, and Manufacturing as a Service (MaaS), and included strategy, business development, program management, and solution architecture.

Gerhard Riehl is Head of Pricing and Proposals for production and export at Airbus Defence and Space, based in Munich, Germany. Before that he was a commercial contract manager at Airbus.

Mark Shafer is the Senior Vice President of Revenue and Profit Management at Walt Disney World based in Orlando, FL. Previously he was Senior Director of International Revenue Management and Pricing at Continental Airlines. He is also a member of the editorial board of the *Journal of Revenue and Pricing Management*.

Todd Snelgrove is a Founding Partner of Experts in Value, and was previously a Vice President at ABB, and a Global Vice President of Value at SKF, a leading global industrial engineering company. He has been published in various academic journals, served as keynote speaker at numerous global conferences, and supports executive MBA classes at schools such as Northwestern University, Evanston, IL; London Business School, UK; and the International Institute for Management Development, Lausanne, Switzerland.

Jose Vela is Director of Pricing at Spandex, a leading trade supplier to sign making, digital, and display industries. Previously he held general management positions at Spandex and other companies.

Part 1
Introduction

1 Introduction

Implementing pricing strategies

Andreas Hinterhuber and Stephan M. Liozu

The implementation of pricing strategies is not easy. As the chapters in this book show, even small organizational changes can be very hard to implement. What looks simple from the outside is difficult when viewed from inside organizations where entrenched habits, a bias towards the status quo, and risk aversion work against change, including change for the better. Pricing strategy implementation has two broad aims: (1) behavioral change and (2) an improvement in company performance. The implementation of pricing strategies, i.e. the achievement of consistent behavioral change that improves firm performance, entails a true organizational transformation. The following provides an illustration.

The digital transformation of Adobe: the implementation of an innovative pricing strategy

Adobe, a US$9 billion software company, is an excellent example of a successful digital transformation, where the implementation of a new pricing strategy is the central element. In 2011, more than 80 percent of the company's sales were product-based: the company sold perpetual licenses to customers. In 2018, close to 90 percent of the company's sales were subscriptions: the company predominantly sold usage rights to customers. The move from products to subscriptions is driven both by a strong customer orientation – subscription sales allow immediate product updates, as opposed to product sales that are driven by release cycles – as well as by a healthy profit objective. Mark Garrett, CFO of Adobe, comments, "We were driving revenue growth by raising our average selling price—either through straight price increases or through moving people up the product ladder. That wasn't a sustainable approach" (Sprague, 2015, pp. 1–2). The implementation of the new pricing strategy follows a substantial internal and external analysis. Again, Garrett comments,

> We spent hours knee-deep in Excel spreadsheets modeling this out. We literally covered the boardroom with pricing and unit models. Through this discussion, which took about a year, we saw that we could manage through it and that we, our customers, and our shareholders would come out on the other side much better off.
>
> (Sprague, 2015, p. 2)

The digital transformation and the implementation of the new pricing strategy are delivering results: from 2011 to 2018 sales revenues doubled and operating margins increased from 26 percent to 32 percent. This successful implementation of the new pricing strategy can be read in light of an organizational capability that is relevant in the context of digital transformations: digital business agility, consisting of (1) hyperawareness, (2) informed decision making, and (3) fast execution (Wade, 2015). In the context of the implementation of the new pricing strategy, Adobe fundamentally changed its culture, structure, sales force capabilities and incentives, communication to customers, and communication to investors (Gupta and Barley, 2015). The case of Adobe illustrates another principle of a successful pricing strategy implementation. Major structural changes in pricing strategy such as the one implemented by Adobe in the context of a digital transformation require significant, upfront communication to customers. Small changes, ranging anywhere from 1 percent to 3 percent (Monroe, Rikala, and Somervuori, 2015) do not. Companies simply need the confidence to implement them without a blink.

Finally, it is noteworthy that the average selling price to customers increased from about US$30 per month under perpetual licensing to about US$37 under subscriptions (Gupta and Barley, 2015) – despite the stated intent of the company's CFO of not increasing company profitability via price increases. The Adobe case study, therefore, offers many fascinating lessons; a few deserve to be highlighted. First, innovation in pricing allows for customer satisfaction and profits conjointly (Hinterhuber and Liozu, 2014). Second, an understanding of business-to-business (B2B) customer psychology allows the company to favorably influence customer perceptions of value and price without actually lowering the price (Hinterhuber, 2015b). Third, pricing strategy implementation is all about action, the confidence to overcome internal and external resistance in order to get things done (Liozu, 2015).

Contents of the book

This book is one of the few books – possibly the only book – exclusively dedicated to the topic of pricing strategy implementation. This book examines implementation from three different angles: first, the organizational perspective. Leaders in organizations provide frameworks in order to direct and structure pricing strategy implementation. Second, the sales force. The sales force clearly is the critical link where pricing excellence manifests itself most visibly. Third, marketing. The role of marketing is changing: from supporting the sales function to creating new markets, from understanding customer needs to contributing to influencing customer purchase criteria, and from communicating product features to documenting and quantifying customer value. In the context of pricing strategy implementation, value quantification is arguably one of the critical responsibilities where sales managers depend on the marketing function to develop tools, case studies, and best practices for quantifying and documenting customer value. These three perspectives on pricing strategy implementation thus provide the basic structure of the book.

Structure of the book

Part I, "Introduction," contains this introductory chapter by Andreas Hinterhuber and Stephan M. Liozu.

Part II, "Aligning the organization around pricing strategy implementation," contains several chapters that address the organizational capabilities needed to implement pricing strategies.

In Chapter 2, "Implementing pricing strategies: The frameworks to drive profits by pricing actions," Andreas Hinterhuber discusses a series of frameworks that guide the process of pricing strategy implementation. A common thread of these frameworks is that they recognize the challenges of achieving behavioral change at the individual level: pricing strategy implementation is an instance of managing organizational change.

In Chapter 3, "Elevating the cost of doing nothing: An interview with Mark Shafer," Andreas Hinterhuber, Evandro Pollono, and Mark Shafer discuss the implementation pricing and revenue management at Disney from the perspective of the company's Senior Vice President of Revenue and Profit Management. Highlights of this interview include the comment that "the cost of doing nothing is not zero," suggesting that elevating the cost of inaction can overcome internal resistance to change and may thus be an important instrument for articulating the need for change. The interview also highlights the characteristics at the level of individual decision makers that facilitate the implementation of pricing and revenue management and reminds us of the ever-present, frequently invisible biases in this process. Finally, the interview illuminates the importance of data and analytics as the basis for rational decision making in order to drive profits via pricing and revenue management.

Part III, "Pricing strategy implementation: The role of the sales force" contains several chapters that highlight the role of the sales force in pricing strategy implementation.

In Chapter 4, "The role of the sales force in pricing strategy implementation," Andreas Hinterhuber and Frank Cespedes explore capabilities and personality traits of sales managers in implementing pricing strategy. Cespedes suggests that buyer expectations influence sales manager capabilities; and indeed, value quantification capabilities at the level of individual sales managers are the result of buyers demanding or, at least, responding positively to quantified value propositions. Cespedes then suggests that the search for personality traits linked to sales manager effectiveness is inherently flawed: effective traits depend strongly on product type, customer type, and price range so that, in the end, all traits can be, under different circumstances, effective. Although this is arguably true, current research suggests that a restricted set of personality traits is associated with sales manager effectiveness. In terms of behaviors, this interview sheds light on critical elements of value-based selling – understanding customer needs, customer segmentation, customer selection, value proposition development, value-based pricing, and value quantification – that are critically important also in the context of pricing strategy implementation. A critical aspect of pricing strategy implementation is sales force incentives, which should be margin-based and reward price performance. In practice, this frequently is not the case: most sales force incentives are based on volume.

In Chapter 5, "The strategic account manager as ecosystem captain: Driving profits via pricing," Andreas Hinterhuber and Bernard Quancard explore in detail the changing role of the strategic account manager (SAM). In the future, Quancard suggests, the SAM will be an ecosystem captain capable of managing complex relationships and teams, of organizing data, and of telling stories with analytics. The role of the SAM with respect to pricing is a function of the customer relationship. Quancard suggests the following alternatives: a purely transactional relationship (no role for the SAM), a supplier shortlist (a very limited role for the SAM), standard solutions (a consultative role for the SAM), and trusted advisor relationships (SAMs drive pricing). In this view, SAMs should have value quantification capabilities, but not necessarily pricing capabilities, which SAMs should be able to access – via, for example, a dedicated pricing function – but are not necessarily part of the capabilities that SAMs should master. Incentives do play a role with respect to strategy implementation: Hinterhuber and Quancard suggest that the compensation of a SAM should be based on five items: activities, competencies, intermediary results, sales/gross margins, and the amount of quantified business value that the SAM has created. Finally, Quancard also points toward emerging capabilities of the SAM highlighting three capabilities: diagnostic skills, value innovation, and transformation agent. In sum, this superb interview is a must read for all sales and account managers who are looking for ways to expand their impact in organizations.

In Chapter 6, "Designing sales force compensation to improve pricing execution," Stephan M. Liozu discusses the results of qualitative interviews with 12 pricing executives regarding the challenging topic of changing sales force compensation to drive pricing execution. This chapter proposes the modification of compensation plans in steps over time with a strong focus on change management. It proposes practical ways to include pricing metrics in an overall compensation basket while underscoring the need to model past versus future compensation impact with each sales rep. Modifying sales force compensation can be one of the most explosive and emotional topics of every pricing transformation. It needs to be prepared with care and intention.

Part IV, "Pricing strategy implementation: The role of marketing," contains several chapters that highlight the role of marketing in pricing strategy implementation.

In Chapter 7, "Implementing pricing strategies by developing and implementing effective discounting practices," Evandro Pollono and Jose Vela also discuss the evolving capabilities of sales managers. Vela, like Quancard, stresses analytical skills and the emerging role of sales managers as transformation agents. With respect to pricing strategy implementation, Vela highlights the important role of discounting guidelines and customer segmentation. Managers should analyze transaction-level data in order to develop discounting guidelines that can serve as a guide and benchmark for sales manager pricing behavior.

In Chapter 8, "Designing and executing your B2B segmentation," Stephan M. Liozu and Katie Richardson highlight the various implications of designing a B2B segmentation process. This chapter first proposes a refresher of what segmentation is. Second, it lists six best practices on how to make segmentation a success exercise in any B2B organization. The authors then focus on the need to operationalize the segmentation in the go-to-market process to really reap the benefit of such a challenging exercise. The benefits are in the execution of superior commercial strategies guided by the segmentation process. Managers often struggle with the execution of segmentation in their business. This chapter focuses on critical practical steps they must make to get to the next level of marketing and commercial success.

In Chapter 9, "Training programs to boost pricing execution," Stephan M. Liozu discusses the importance of redesigning training programs to make pricing execution programs impactful. The author posits that traditional lecture-style training programs are not the most optimal way to train experienced sales professionals. The chapter starts with a four-step approach to getting started with the design of a unique and disruptive training program. Then the author proposes practical learning and training tips to increase the level of absorption and stickiness of pricing-related knowledge. The key is to focus on the blend of training methods, delivery style, and diversified content. These tips can be immediately included in your ongoing pricing transformational roadmap.

In Chapter 10, "Implementing a structured pricing strategy approach," Ingo Hennecke proposes a practical application of John Kotter's change management framework to pricing transformation. The author goes through every step and proposes practical recommendations on how to apply the process. This chapter reinforces the need for deep change management focus to make pricing transformation and pricing execution successful.

Part V, "Implementing pricing strategies that win deals," contains chapters discussing how managers can identify the specific price points that win deals profitably.

In Chapter 11, "Pricing large deals: Insights into capabilities and tools that help to win large deals profitably," Andreas Hinterhuber discusses how value quantification and mapping of B2B purchase criteria can help to win large deals profitably. Offers are frequently concentrated in industrial markets: winning the 4–10 percent of deals that account for 80 percent of revenues is thus very important. Value quantification is the process of translating competitive advantages into quantified, monetary, customer-specific value (Hinterhuber, 2017). This idea is explored in several subsequent book chapters by Hinterhuber, Snelgrove, Liozu, and Marshall. Value quantification thus identifies the total value or maximum price of an offer. B2B purchase criteria mapping, by contrast, examines the impact of specific price points on the likelihood of winning the deal. By performing both value quantification and B2B purchase criteria mapping, industrial sellers can substantially increase the likelihood of winning large deals profitably.

In Chapter 12, "Pricing to win: A framework for strategic bid decision making," Gerhard Riehl offers a further perspective on deal pricing. Riehl outlines four steps: understanding customer demand (customer stakeholders, customer budget, customer value), understanding competition, value quantification and measurement, and, finally, bid pricing. Chapters 12 and 13 by Riehl and Hinterhuber are complementary, with Riehl stressing to a larger degree the need to understand customer stakeholders and customer budget constraints. Both chapters stress that the application of a structured process and the use of tools (value quantification, purchase criteria mapping, stakeholder analysis, competitor analysis) increase both win rates and selling prices.

Value quantification is the topic of the next two chapters. First, in Chapter 13, "Value quantification: Processes and best practices to document and quantify value in B2B," Andreas Hinterhuber presents the results of an empirical survey on value quantification capabilities in European and US-based B2B companies. This chapter presents five key steps that can guide managers in industrial companies to quantify value: generation of customer insight, value creation through meaningful differentiation and collaboration, value proposition development, value quantification, and implementation/documentation. This chapter also highlights several company case studies of quantified customer value propositions; SKF, Tieto, and SAP among them.

SKF is also the subject of the subsequent chapter. Todd Snelgrove, the former Chief Value Officer at SKF, highlights the role of quantified value propositions in the context of value-based selling and value-based pricing. In Chapter 14, "Implementing pricing strategies via quantified value propositions," Snelgrove emphasizes that quantified value propositions are a key element to shift B2B purchasers from price to value. Quantified value propositions are either total value of ownership calculations (Snelgrove, 2012) or value quantification tools (Hinterhuber, 2015a). For sales managers, value-based selling requires two conditions: ability and motivation. The ability to sell value depends on the ability to conceptualize value in a way that resonates with customers, on processes encouraging a focus on value, on the availability of value-selling tools, on initial training, and on ongoing experience in value selling. The motivation to sell value is a function of sales force compensation, of the ability to build long-term collaborative relationships with customers where both parties are committed to creating mutually beneficial value, of a company culture led by a strong CEO committed to value-based selling and, finally, of customers that recognize the opportunity to work collaboratively with suppliers. This chapter thus explores the multiple facets that companies can and should control in order to implement value-based selling and value quantification. The chapter also vividly illustrates the difference between given price savings and total cost of ownership savings of equal amount. If the total cost of ownership savings occur year after year and if price savings occur just once, then the effect of the former will by far outweigh the benefits of the latter.

In Chapter 15, "Adopt value selling: Best practices to drive sustainable organizational change," Peyton Marshall outlines the necessity to have proper process and tools to drive the implementation of value-selling projects. Standardized processes and templates help with the systematic adoption of new methodologies, especially when they impact the daily routine of salespeople. The author proposes four considerations that are essential in the design and execution of value-selling pilot projects. He then describes a simple checklist that is effective in driving initial sales adoption of value selling at a time before there is evidence of success.

In Chapter 16, "Executing price control in five simple steps," Mitchell D. Lee makes a strong argument that taking control of pricing by consolidating information, formalizing policies, and standardizing language and practices should be your first step toward systematically increasing an organization's growth and profitability. To do this, they offer five steps to help control price using technology. The authors make a strong case for the use of pricing systems to improve the level of pricing control and therefore the level of pricing execution. With technology as a key enabler of pricing execution, teams can focus on selling and rely on relevant pricing guidelines to steer them in the right direction.

Finally, the book finishes with a very practical list of eight best practices to improve pricing execution. Chapter 17, "Eight best practices to improve pricing execution," written by Stephan M. Liozu, provides specific actions managers can use to improve their level of focus on pricing execution. Lots of people discuss execution or think they are good at it. Until you implement these practices, you might not be executing well!

This book is thus a call to action highlighting how managers and leaders in organizations can change organizations so that performance improves as a result of pricing. We hope that readers will heed.

References

Gupta, S., & Barley, L. (2015). Reinventing Adobe. Harvard Business School Case Study, 9-514-066, 1–17.
Hinterhuber, A. (2015a). Value quantification: the next challenge for B2B selling. In A. Hinterhuber & S. Liozu (Eds.), *Pricing and the Sales Force* (pp. 20–32). New York: Routledge.
Hinterhuber, A. (2015b). Violations of rational choice principles in pricing decisions. *Industrial Marketing Management*, 47, 65–74.
Hinterhuber, A. (2017). Value quantification capabilities in industrial markets. *Journal of Business Research*, 76, 163–178.
Hinterhuber, A., & Liozu, S. (2014). Is innovation in pricing your next source of competitive advantage? *Business Horizons*, 57(3), 413–423.
Liozu, S. (2015). Pricing superheroes: How a confident sales team can influence firm performance. *Industrial Marketing Management*, 47, 26–38.
Monroe, K. B., Rikala, V.-M., & Somervuori, O. (2015). Examining the application of behavioral price research in business-to-business markets. *Industrial Marketing Management*, 47, 17–25.
Snelgrove, T. (2012). Value pricing when you understand your customers: Total cost of ownership – past, present and future. *Journal of Revenue & Pricing Management*, 11(1), 76–80.
Sprague, K. (2015). *Interview: Reborn in the Cloud* (White paper). McKinsey & Company.
Wade, M. (2015). *Digital Business Transformation: A Conceptual Framework Global Center for Digital Business Transformation*. Lausanne, Switzerland: IMD.

Part 2
Aligning the organization around pricing strategy implementation

2 Implementing pricing strategies
The frameworks to drive profits by pricing actions

Andreas Hinterhuber

Introduction

Implementation is the difficult part of the pricing. Pricing projects typically have the following phases: (1) diagnostics, (2) pricing strategy development, (3) pricing pilot tests, and (4) implementation. The first three phases typically take place in well-defined environments: the diagnostics phase is all about data collection, the strategy development phase is about defining goals and major pricing initiatives, and, finally, the pilot testing phase is about improving the strategy by conducting pilot tests on a limited scale. The implementation phase is where many companies struggle. Implementation is not easy: internal resistance, customer objections, changes in customer preferences, new competitors, unexpected competitive actions, and leadership changes are all elements that can prevent even the best designed pricing strategy from coming to life. Implementation is all about motivating people in organizations to do things that they did not do before. Models that guarantee fail-safe implementation clearly do not exist. However, what research has to offer are models of organizational change management that spell out the levers that managers can activate in order to increase the likelihood of strategy implementation. In this chapter I will present salient models, discuss their theoretical basis, and highlight their applicability to pricing strategy implementation. To managers, these models offer guidelines to implement pricing strategies. To researchers, these models offer an opportunity to conduct further studies on those elements that so far lack an empirical validation.

Frameworks of pricing strategy implementation

Researchers have produced dozens of models that highlight how organizations can achieve lasting change. In Figure 2.1 and in the following I present some salient models with a short description of their empirical basis.

The 8-step change model

The 8-step change model by Kotter (1995) is arguably one of the most widely known frameworks to implement organizational change. The empirical basis is weak and it does not appear that the main propositions of the model are based on qualitative or quantitative research. There is, however, numerous anecdotal evidence supporting the model.

Managers who wish to transform organizations should do the following (Kotter 1995): they need to establish a sense of urgency, they need to form powerful guiding coalitions, they need to establish a compelling vision, they need to communicate this vision, they

12 Andreas Hinterhuber

Author		Model	Qualitative Research	Quantitative Research	Pricing Part of Scope
1995	KOTTER	8-step change model	−	−	−
2002	ULRICH, KERR, AND ASHKENAS	Change Acceleration Process	+	−	−
2010	HEATH AND HEATH	Switch model	−	−	−
2011	KELLER AND PRICE	McKinsey influence model	+	+	−
1993	DICHTER, GAGNON AND ALEXANDER	Transformation triangle	+	−	−
2008	KELLOGG	Free-spaces theory	+	−	−
2015	LIOZU	5C model	+	+	+

Figure 2.1 Frameworks to implement pricing strategies.

need to remove the inevitable obstacles to change, they need quick wins able to demonstrate that pricing works, they need to build on these quick wins, and they need to, finally, institutionalize the new approach to pricing in their culture (see Figure 2.2).

The scope of the model is broad and it has, like nearly all models discussed herein, been designed with a strategy and leadership, and not a pricing, perspective. Nevertheless, there is evidence that this model has been fruitfully employed to successfully guide pricing strategy implementation. Schneider Electric, a global energy management company, is using Kotter's model to drive profits via pricing (Ingham 2013).

The Change Acceleration Process

The Change Acceleration Process (CAP) model was originally developed at General Electric under Jack Welch as a tool to implement a key initiative – Jack Welch's Work-Out sessions (Ulrich, Kerr, and Ashkenas 2002). The fundamental premise of the CAP model is this: successful and unsuccessful organizational change efforts have equally good technical solutions or approaches; what distinguishes successful from unsuccessful organizational change programs is the acceptance of ideas and not their technical merits. Key focus of the model is thus building acceptance of ideas to drive organizational change.

The model has the following seven components: leading change, creating a shared need, shaping a vision, mobilizing commitment, making change last, monitoring progress, and, finally, systems and structures. Figure 2.3 provides an overview.

The seven elements of the model are, in detail:

- Leading change refers to the need to have a champion providing visible, active, public commitment to the change.
- Creating a shared need refers to framing change by highlighting the opportunity of changing or the risks of not changing; opportunities and risks should be based on data, best practices, or customer demands.

MAIN STEPS		KEY ACTIVITIES
Establishing a Sense of Urgency	1	Examining competitive realities Identifying crises or major opportunities
Forming a Powerful Guiding Coalition	2	Assembling a group with enough power Encouraging the group to work together
Creating a Vision	3	Creating a vision to direct the change Developing implementation strategies
Communicating the Vision	4	Using every vehicle to communicate Teaching new behaviors by example
Empowering Others to Act on the Vision	5	Eliminating obstacles; changing structure Encouraging risk taking
Planning for and Creating Short-Term Wins	6	Planning and creating key improvements Rewarding employees involved
Consolidating Improvements and Producing Still More Change	7	Using increased credibility to changing structures that don't fit; adding projects
Institutionalizing New Approaches	8	Articulating the connections between the new behaviors and corporate success

Figure 2.2 The 8-step change model.
(*Source*: adapted from Kotter 1995)

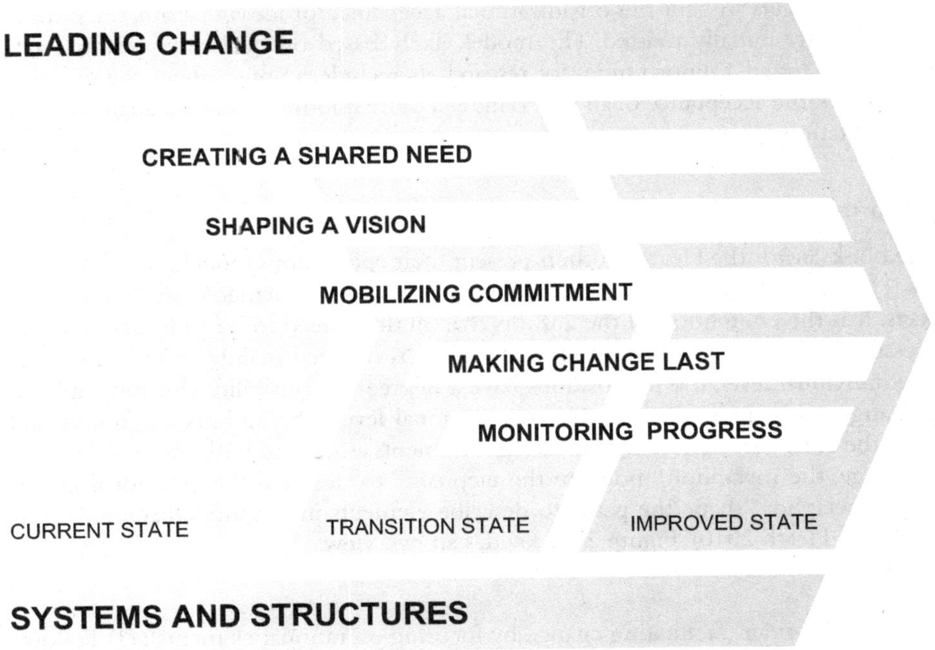

LEADING CHANGE

CREATING A SHARED NEED

SHAPING A VISION

MOBILIZING COMMITMENT

MAKING CHANGE LAST

MONITORING PROGRESS

CURRENT STATE   TRANSITION STATE   IMPROVED STATE

SYSTEMS AND STRUCTURES

Figure 2.3 The Change Acceleration Process.
(*Source*: adapted from Ulrich, Kerr, and Ashkenas 2002)

- Shaping a vision refers to describing the desired outcome of change processes in behavioral terms that are clear and widely understood. In the CAP model all change is behavioral. Managers thus need to translate the vision of the change in behaviors that they want to observe in any given context.
- Mobilizing commitment refers to the emotional investment of participants to make the change and demand management attention in order to make the change work. Listing key stakeholders and mapping their degree of support (from strongly against to strongly supportive) is a first step in mobilizing commitment. Causes of resistance to change can be analyzed by mapping technical, political, and cultural factors (Tichy 1982).
- Making change last requires that change efforts are integrated with other strategic initiatives so that a momentum builds for the initiative. As a result, organizations thus acquire a new way of life. The organizational change thus leads to a permanently different way of action.
- Monitoring progress implies developing performance indicators that benchmark change efforts against predetermined targets so that corrective action can be taken in case of deviations from desired courses of action.
- Systems and structures refer to the supporting organizational infrastructure that needs to be aligned with the change program in order to reinforce the desired outcome. Incentive systems, competency development programs, communication programs, staffing programs, IT systems, and structural adjustments are factors that should be considered in this context. As a start, managers can map current systems and assess to which degree current systems and structures facilitate or hinder the organizational change program.

In summary: GE's CAP model is based on research in a large, diversified company and highlights salient elements of successful organizational change management programs by enabling managers to gain the organizational acceptance of ideas that are, since they are new, frequently initially resisted. The model, likely based on qualitative research at GE, has not been tested. Opportunities for researchers include, among others, the question to which extent the acceptance of an idea is indeed more important than its quality regarding implementation success.

Switch model

In the book *Switch*, the Heath brothers present their eponymous model consisting of three parts (Heath and Heath 2010): rational elements, emotional elements, and environmental aspects. It is the contention of the authors that all three need to be addressed in order to successfully implement change. While the model is directed mainly at achieving change at the individual level, the propositions have a degree of plausibility also for implementing change across individuals at the organizational level. The authors use the metaphor "direct the rider" for describing the rational elements associated with successfully managing change, the metaphor "motivate the elephant" to describe the emotional elements, and the metaphor "shape the path" to describe elements in the immediate environment (Heath and Heath 2010). Figure 2.4 provides an overview.

In brief:

- Direct the rider (facilitating change by focusing on rational elements): (1) Follow the bright spots. Adopt a solution focus – focus on what is working already now. (2) Script the critical moves. Set simple and specific behavioral goals. Clarity reduces resistance.

DIRECT THE RIDER
- FOLLOW THE BRIGHT SPOTS: Adopt a solution focus – focus on what is working already now.
- SCRIPT THE CRITICAL MOVES: Set simple and specific behavioral goals. Clarity reduces resistance.
- POINT TO THE DESTINATION: Depict a vivid image of the future and set unambiguous yes/no goals.

MOTIVATE THE ELEPHANT
- FIND THE FEELING: create positive emotions and appeal to a person's desired identity.
- SHRINK THE CHANGE: achieve small, visible goals (quick wins) to grow a sense of confidence. Focus on what has been achieved.
- GROW YOUR PEOPLE: Align the change with a person's desired self image.
Adopt a growth mindset and reward efforts: not only results.

SHAPE THE PATH
- TWEAK THE ENVIRONMENT:
Design the environment so that desired behavior becomes easier and undesired behavior impossible.
- BUILD HABITS:
Develop action triggers that automate behaviors: use checklists.
- RALLY THE HERD:
Build supportive peer groups.
Create positive competitions to implement change.

Figure 2.4 The Switch model.
(*Source*: adapted from Heath and Heath 2010)

(3) Point to the destination. Depict a vivid image of the future and set unambiguous yes/no goals.
- Motivate the elephant (obtaining emotional commitment to the change): (1) Find the feeling. Create positive emotions and appeal to a person's desired identity. (2) Shrink the change. Achieve small, visible goals (quick wins) to grow a sense of confidence. Focus on what has been achieved. (3) Grow your people. Align the change with a person's desired self-image. Adopt a growth mindset and reward efforts, not only results.
- Tweak the path (facilitate change by influencing the environment): (1) Tweak the environment. Design the environment so that desired behavior becomes easier and undesired behavior impossible. (2) Build habits. Develop action triggers that automate behaviors; use checklists. (3) Rally the herd. Build supportive peer groups. Create positive competitions to implement change.

In sum, the switch model stresses three key aspects: providing a rational base for implementing the change, obtaining emotional commitment, and influencing the immediate environment. Since the evidence is largely anecdotal, opportunities to test the model abound. Examining the identity model (March 1994) and its relevance in the context of implementing organizational change looks particularly promising.

McKinsey influence model

McKinsey has developed a model of organizational transformation that has been tested in a variety of empirical surveys with managers: the influence model (Basford, Schaninger, and Viruleg 2015; Claret, Mauger, and Roegner 2006; Keller and Price 2011).

The model has four components: (1) framing – top management provides direction and support, (2) enabling – managers develop the skills that are required to implement the change, (3) motivating – managers provide the motivation to change, and (4) follow-up – managers reinforce the desired change through feedback and learning (see Figure 2.5).

The elements of the model in detail:

- Framing: leaders act as role models for the change efforts and interact with the organization on the rationale for the change. As a result, employees should be able to say, "I can see leaders behaving differently."
- Enabling: managers develop the tools and skills to enable employees to implement the required change. As a result, employees should be able to state, "I know what I need to do and I have the skills to do it."
- Motivating: managers ensure that employees are actually motivated to implement desired changes. Of importance here are rewards, recognitions, and performance consequences of implementing desired changes. As a result, employees should say, "I and my associates are committed to change."
- Follow-up: managers adjust the organizational structure so that monitoring and feedback systems reinforce desired changes. As a result, employees should be able to say, "Our processes and systems are geared toward making the change stick."

The central premise of the model is that individual and collective behavior change only as a result of working simultaneously on the four elements of leadership (providing direction), capability building (enabling the change), motivation (providing incentives), and monitoring (comparing actual to target behaviors). The model is simple, but has empirical support. For managers the model thus offers a framework that can guide the organizational transformation that changes in pricing strategies frequently entail.

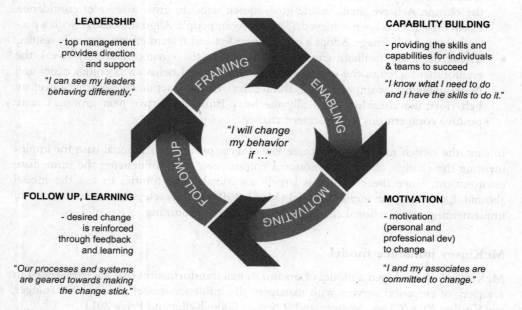

Figure 2.5 The McKinsey influence model.

(Source: adapted from Keller and Price 2011)

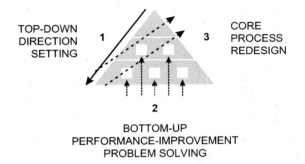

Figure 2.6 The transformation triangle.

(*Source*: adapted from Dichter, Gagnon, and Alexander 1993)

The transformation triangle

Earlier research, also at McKinsey, has produced an equally simply and plausible model for strategy implementation: the transformation triangle (Dichter, Gagnon, and Alexander 1993). The goal here as well is to achieve lasting behavioral change that improves performance. To do this, managers need to coordinate activities along three axes: top down, bottom up, and across core processes (see Figure 2.6). Change along the three axes should be focused, with a limited scope being preferred to a broad scope; integrated, in order that change efforts reinforce each other; balanced, giving equal attention to each axis; and team-based (Dichter, Gagnon, and Alexander 1993).

In detail:

- Top-down initiatives refer to consistent and clear direction settings by top management.
- Bottom-up initiatives refer to enabling a large number of persons to implement fundamentally new ways of operating by changing performance targets, work practices, capabilities, and employee involvement.
- Core process redesign refers to linking people and activities in new ways so as to substantially improve performance.

Figure 2.7 provides a detailed overview of the activities that managers can implement along each of the three axes.

The free spaces theory

The free spaces theory of Kellogg (2008) uses social movement theory to examine the conditions that favor the implementation of real change. The author compares and contrasts changing work practices following the introduction of new regulations in two hospitals via ethnographic research.

A core finding of the theory is that even small changes are very difficult to implement. The author makes the point by examining a reduction in working hours – demanded by regulators – in large hospitals. This change clearly is positive for employees, yet it contrasts prevailing institutional norms that favor dedication and very long working hours. The main finding of the free spaces theory is changes in institutionalized work practices occur

TOP-DOWN DIRECTION SETTING AND CULTURE SHAPING		BOTTOM-UP PERFOMANCE IMPROVEMENT		CORE PROCESS REDESIGN	
VISION	Broad agreement in management ranks; clearly and compellingly used for decision making and priority setting	GOAL SETTING (HOW MUCH)	Ambitious goals with clear milestones, drawing on internal and external benchmarks	PERFOMANCE OBJECTIVES	Targets reflect breakpoints based on value to the customer
LEADERSHIP AGENDA	Top group devotes substantial time to reinforcing agenda and sets clear expectations for others to do likewise	BENCHMARKING	Driven by line managers and part of ongoing management process	REDESIGN PROCESS	Clean-sheet redesign questioning fundamental assumption underlying how work is done
PROCESS DESIGN	"Home-grown" process with mutually reinforcing thrusts and clear milestones; tied to goals and vision	PROBLEM-SOLVING METHODOLOGY	Wide array of tools available and applied flexibly, based on need	CHANGE MENEGEMENT	Clearly defined program for skill building (e.g., recruting/selection, training, career-path management)
COMMUNICATIONS	Communications system thet includes feedback loops and measurement	INVOLVEMENT	Perfomance-oriented involvment pervasive and built into management system	SHARED VALUES	Aggressive communication by senior management to reinforce new values
TRAINING	Training fully adapted to support new skills; significant and delivered by line	IMPLEMENTATION DRIVER	Line	MEASURING AND MONITORING	Perfomance indicators are incorporated in evaluation procedures
MEASUREMENT	Series of transaction-level measures; "cascading" measures throughout organization (i.e. "right numbers to right people"); regular review of benchmarks	WORK REDESIGN (e.g., redesigning jobs, roles, incentives, information systems)	Integrated redesign at many key units/levels; often cerried out by incumbents		

Figure 2.7 The three axes for implementing organizational change.

(*Source*: adapted from Dichter, Gagnon, and Alexander 1993) only when free spaces exist where employees and change-oriented managers can interact freely without interference from managers that defend the status quo (Kellogg 2008). Free spaces enable change-oriented employees and managers to develop a new collective identity, new capabilities, and an oppositional identity defined by new working practices. A central finding is that this development of new practices, new capabilities, and new identities occurs only when reform-oriented managers are isolated from managers defending the status quo: free spaces allow experimentation, learning, and the development of a new collective identity.

This research adds an important finding to organizational research. The current literature is in fact not fully conclusive on how to achieve large-scale organizational transformation. The models discussed so far and other pertinent research suggest that companies can in fact transform their core (Bower and Christensen 1995); other studies suggest that fundamental organizational transformation requires that a separate organizational unit is set up ("skunk works") where the change is implemented (Kumar, Scheer, and Kotler 2000). Kellogg (2008) suggests that a middle ground exists: companies can change the core by creating an empty space within.

In the context of pricing, this empty core can thus be used to implement new approaches to pricing: value-based pricing, value quantification, value-based selling, new discounting practices, and new approaches to market and customer segmentation.

The 5C model

Liozu (2015a) developed a model dealing with the organizational change related to pricing – the 5C model. It is the only model that has been tested via qualitative research (Liozu et al. 2012), that has been tested via quantitative research (Liozu, Hinterhuber, and Somers 2014), and that deals exclusively with pricing. The 5Cs are champions, center-led pricing organization, capabilities, confidence, and change management capacity (see Figure 2.8).

In detail:

- Champions: senior executives typically do not have an active interest in pricing. Without their support pricing initiatives are, as virtually all models discussed emphasize, bound to fail. Champions are senior managers that actively promote the pricing function, provide support for pricing, remove obstacles, and channel organizational energy toward driving profits via pricing.
- Center-led pricing organization: a center-led pricing organization attempts to combine the advantages of a decentralized approach to price decision-making (e.g., better insights into customer willingness to pay) with the advantages of a centralized approach (e.g., expertise, standardization). A center-led pricing organization typically consists of a central pricing function (e.g., a chief pricing officer) supporting decentralized sales, and marketing managers with behavioral guidelines and decision rules.
- Capabilities: organizational pricing capabilities can be measured and in fact have a positive effect on company performance (Liozu and Hinterhuber 2014). Pricing capabilities essentially measure the extent to which pricing decision makers consider the three critical dimensions of pricing (Hinterhuber 2004): the customer, i.e., customer willingness to pay, customer price elasticity, and quantified customer value; the competition, i.e., competitive price trends and offer configurations; and, finally, the company, i.e., pricing processes, tools, and cost structures.

Figure 2.8 The 5C model.
(*Source*: adapted from Liozu 2015a)

- Confidence: new approaches to pricing, the implementation of value-based pricing, for example, require confidence. Confidence is a soft trait, an attitude: empirical research, however, clearly shows that small changes in sales manager confidence have a substantial impact on company performance (Liozu 2015b; Liozu and Hinterhuber 2013). Senior managers thus should aim to develop confidence in sales, marketing, and pricing managers.
- Change management: the organizational change capacity is the ability to continuously learn, adapt to, and initiate changes (Judge and Blocker 2008). The change capability is linked to a culture that promotes accountability and innovation, to leaders who are trustworthy, to followers who trust leaders, to effective communication, and to organizational learning (Liozu 2015a).

In sum, the 5C model is a robust, empirically tested model that spells out the main levers on how to implement the organizational transformation associated with pricing.

The map and the territory

Models are like maps – they help to navigate new and unknown territory. Pricing strategies fail, typically not because of a flaw in their design, but because of the implementation that stalls somewhere in the organization. The maps presented here offer a way to navigate the terrain: no map can replace a sound understanding of local circumstances, but good maps do help. To managers these maps thus offer guidance in the strategy implementation. To researchers these maps and the relatively large white open spaces of *terra incognita* offer numerous opportunities to investigate the circumstances under which small and large changes in a company's pricing strategy succeed or fail.

References

Basford, T., B. Schaninger, and E. Viruleg. (2015). *The Science of Organizational Transformations*. New York: McKinsey & Company.

Bower, J. L., and C. M. Christensen. (1995). "Disruptive Technologies: Catching the Wave." *Harvard Business Review*, 73 (1), 43–53.

Claret, J., P. Mauger, and E. Roegner. (2006). "Managing a Marketing and Sales Transformation." *The McKinsey Quarterly*, 76, 111–21.

Dichter, S., C. Gagnon, and A. Alexander. (1993). "Memo to a CEO: Leading Organizational Transformations." *The McKinsey Quarterly*, 1 (Spring) 89–106.

Heath, C., and D. Heath. (2010). *Switch: How to Change Things When Change Is Hard*. New York: Random House.

Hinterhuber, A. (2004). "Towards Value-Based Pricing – An Integrative Framework for Decision Making." *Industrial Marketing Management*, 33 (8), 765–78.

Ingham, G. (2013). "Make the Most of Your Crisis." Paper presented at the Professional Pricing Society, Atlanta, GA.

Judge, W. Q., and C. P. Blocker. (2008). "Organizational Capacity for Change and Strategic Ambidexterity: Flying the Plane While Rewiring It." *European Journal of Marketing*, 42 (9/10), 915–26.

Keller, S., and C. Price. (2011). *Beyond Performance: How Great Organizations Build Ultimate Competitive Advantage*. Hoboken, NJ: John Wiley & Sons.

Kellogg, K. C. (2008). "Not Faking It: Making Real Change in Response to Regulation at Two Surgical Teaching Hospitals." Working paper, MIT Sloan School of Management.

Kotter, J. P. (1995). "Leading Change: Why Transformation Efforts Fail." *Harvard Business Review*, 73 (2), 59–67.

Kumar, N., L. Scheer, and P. Kotler. (2000). "From Market Driven to Market Driving." *European Management Journal*, 18 (2), 129–42.

Liozu, S. (2015a). *The Pricing Journey: The Organizational Transformation Toward Pricing Excellence*. Stanford, CA: Stanford University Press.

Liozu, S. (2015b). "Pricing Superheroes: How a Confident Sales Team Can Influence Firm Performance." *Industrial Marketing Management*, 47, 26–38.

Liozu, S., and A. Hinterhuber. (2014). "Pricing Capabilities: The Design, Development and Validation of a Scale." *Management Decision*, 52 (1), 144–58.

Liozu, S., A. Hinterhuber, S. Perelli, and R. Boland. (2012). "Mindful Pricing: Transforming Organizations through Value-Based Pricing." *Journal of Strategic Marketing*, 20 (3), 1–13.

Liozu, S., A. Hinterhuber, and T. Somers. (2014). "Organizational Design and Pricing Capabilities for Superior Firm Performance." *Management Decision*, 52 (1), 54–78.

Liozu, S. M., and A. Hinterhuber. (2013). "The Confidence Factor in Pricing: Driving Firm Performance." *Journal of Business Strategy*, 34 (4), 11–21.

March, J. (1994). *A Primer on Decision Making: How Decisions Happen*. New York: The Free Press.

Tichy, N. (1982). "Managing Change Strategically: The Technical, Political, and Cultural Keys." *Organizational Dynamics*, 11 (2), 59–80.

Ulrich, D., S. Kerr, and R. Ashkenas. (2002). *The GE Work-Out: How to Implement GE's Revolutionary Method for Busting Bureaucracy and Attacking Organizational Problems – Fast!* New York: McGraw-Hill.

3 Elevating the cost of doing nothing

An interview with Mark Shafer

Andreas Hinterhuber, Evandro Pollono, and Mark Shafer

> This interview discusses the implementation of pricing and revenue management in a large, diversified company – Disney. The interview explores success factors to improve profitability by leveraging the role of analytics in the discipline of revenue management and pricing. The interview also illuminates the characteristics at the level of individual revenue and pricing managers that discriminate between high and average performers. The interview finally points toward the existence of biases in revenue management implementation and reminds that the inability to perceive the inevitable biases severely undermines the ability to improve profitability.

Andreas Hinterhuber:

Mark, today we'll explore insights and key learnings on the implementation of revenue management. Let's begin with your own professional background.

Mark Shafer:

Of course I always need to start off by saying, the views expressed are my own and not necessarily those of the Walt Disney Company. Any analytics strategies or techniques attributed to Disney are not necessarily those that Disney may use in a given situation.

Now to answer your question, my career started with a startup airline called People Express. After three years at People Express Airlines, they were bought out by Continental Airlines. I worked at Continental Airlines for 10 years in both revenue management and pricing roles. I was approached by Walt Disney World 21 years ago to start a revenue management department for their resorts. Disney has always been a leader in innovation; this was a time when the hospitality industry was still in their infancy with revenue management. They were looking for someone with experience from an industry where revenue management was a mature discipline, i.e., the airline industry, in order to bring a new kind of analysis to the company. I started in a traditional hotel revenue management role at Walt Disney World leading the discipline of revenue management.

Like most early adapters we started with something rather simple and it evolved to what it is today. As the models became more sophisticated the value noticeably grew as well. This gave us the opportunity to branch out into other businesses within parks and resorts. As an example, we implemented what we call the "Customer Centric Revenue Management system," which optimized our sales process at the call center to better understand our guests' needs when they are in the process of selecting a resort/room type.

We used this system to ensure we provided the most relevant products for our guests, out of the thousands of possible products we have at Walt Disney World.

Then we introduced revenue management to table service restaurants where it is essential to forecast your turn times. Unlike a resort where it is easy to quantify your inventory by simply counting your rooms, for table service restaurants you need to forecast your turn times so you will know your sellable inventory to appropriately accommodate your guests. To understand your inventory there is a wide array of things to consider: you need to forecast by day of the week, by time of day, by party size, and so on. With this revenue management solution, we were able to make better predictions of our sellable inventory and thus became better at accommodating our guests' needs.

As our successes grew, so did our opportunities. Ten years ago we expanded to applying decision science solutions outside of parks and resorts to other segments of the Walt Disney Company. We moved away from traditional limited-capacity/perishable-inventory revenue management to leveraging applied science to drive a wide array of better business decisions company-wide. Today we develop, implement, and integrate analytical software solutions to support the entire Disney Company to help solve some of our most difficult business problems.

One of our early successes beyond parks was our dynamic pricing and revenue management solution for our Broadway shows such as the *Lion King*. The market took notice when *Lion King* was breaking all kinds of box office receipt records even though it is not the longest running show, nor in the largest theatre, and we do not charge the highest prices on Broadway. Of course, something that cannot be overlooked is that the show is a phenomenal product; clearly this is a key component. However, the software solution we developed to yield manage and dynamically price show tickets certainly played a role in the revenue success. It was fun to see the solution that we developed achieve accolades in articles for the *New York Times*, such as "Ticket Pricing Puts 'Lion King' Atop Broadway's Circle of Life" (Healy, 2014), as well as in other major publications.

We have also developed analytical solutions for our media companies such as ABC, Freeform, ESPN, and our A&E partners as well as Disney Studios, where we expanded applied mathematics to provide insights for marketing ROI, sales optimization, and viewership forecasts. In short, we expanded the scope and definition of revenue management to include leveraging applied science to drive better business decisions, improve long-term profitability, and overall guest/client satisfaction.

Andreas Hinterhuber:

Who recognized the potential for revenue management? Was the initiative driven by middle management, or did it come from the top?

Mark Shafer:

At the very beginning, revenue management was only a forecasting tool to provide operations labor planning insights. Then the VP of finance hired a revenue management team to get revenue management started and to implement it at Walt Disney Resorts. The decision came from senior-level executives who recognized the successes the airlines were having leveraging revenue management; they identified opportunities for success in Walt Disney World by applying it to our resorts as well. I would define our first solution as less science and more business rules, which eventually was replaced with a full science-based solution.

One of the lessons learned that I would share is not to limit yourself to your own industry; rather find the best overall solution and see if you can transform that model into something that might fit your particular industry. At Walt Disney World we didn't just look at hotel-revenue management models; we also looked at airline-revenue management models. Recognizing that the airline models were clearly more sophisticated and probably a better fit for us, we basically took an airline-revenue management model and converted it into a hotel-revenue management model. That was our first real big success in revenue management.

Andreas Hinterhuber:

Revenue management is all about the intelligent use of data. What do you do to instill a sense of passion for data in Disney?

Mark Shafer:

That's a great question, we do a lot of things! To start with, we hold a three-day annual conference on data analytics that we call the Disney Data and Analytics Conference, or DDAC. This year's conference was our sixteenth annual event and it was a big success. The conference has multiple purposes, however it primarily serves to evangelize data analytics across the Walt Disney Company. We actually have a registered trademark for a term that describes just that, we call it Evangalytics®, which is the spreading the gospel of analytics.

The first day of the DDAC is only open to Disney employees. This year we had about 800 internal employees attend of which roughly a third were executives from segments company-wide. During the first day, we share learnings in developing, implementing, and integrating the analytics enterprise-wide. Of course, that's also a great opportunity to evangelize analytics at Disney and share intellectual property because during this time it's all internal employees.

The next two days we open it up to the general public. During these sessions we invite outside speakers as well. This creates two opportunities. First, it provides our Walt Disney Company colleagues an opportunity to hear a perspective from outside the Disney Company. Second, it provides the Walt Disney Company an opportunity to showcase our dedication and efforts in applied science branding us as a leader in the field of analytics. So when the attendees (this year we had a total of about 1300 in attendance) see this massive forum focused around analytics, it demonstrates that applied analytics is a major discipline and investment at the Walt Disney Company.

So when people think about perhaps working for Disney, they may not instinctively think of us as a great company to pursue an analytics career. Normally when you think of Disney, you think of us as a great creative-content, guest-focused company, which we are. But a lot of that requires strong analytics. It's a big component of our success. One of our greatest opportunities is how we use analytics in unique and different ways that are only possible in a varied company like Disney.

Andreas Hinterhuber:

The key differentiating capability that allows Disney to implement revenue management across the different business units, from parks to studios to ESPN, is this focus on analytical capabilities?

Mark Shafer:

Yes, absolutely – and getting full buy-in across the entire organization. Earlier I talked about the value streams of our conference, but there's another value stream in evangelizing analytics. A quote from Jeffrey Ma (who was a keynote speaker at the DDAC 2016) illustrates the point: "There will come a time in analytics where you'll make the right decision but have the wrong outcome." No different than in a football game where the math will recommend you go for a field goal; if you miss the field goal that does not mean you made a bad decision. So, Evangalytics® helps you work through these situations where there is a level of uncertainty. By educating and evangelizing analytics across your company there is buy-in to the value of analytics. So when you have those moments where you made the right decision but had the wrong outcome, you can maintain the buy-in.

Andreas Hinterhuber:

That, Mark, is very well said. You make a distinction between the right process and the right outcome, and you say you would choose the right process 100 percent of the time, even if sometimes you get the wrong outcome.

Mark Shafer:

I want to mention one other piece. We have introduced something new to our DDAC this year, which we call the DDAW – Disney Data and Analytics Women –where we sponsored women college students to attend our conference. The idea is to help them recognize the career opportunities in analytics, as well as realize that Disney is a great company where they can pursue an analytics career. This was our first year with this initiative. The sponsored students had the opportunity to meet and discuss their careers with women executive leaders in analytics from across the Walt Disney Company and it was very well received by both the students and the executives.

Andreas Hinterhuber:

In terms of current research, one fascinating area explores the micro-foundations of pricing, the relationship between individual characteristics and behaviors, and outcomes in pricing: Stephan Liozu and I had the privilege of editing a special issue on this interesting and little explored topic (Hinterhuber & Liozu, 2017). This leads to the next question: What are individual traits that differentiate highly effective from less effective revenue managers? Are there differences across Disney's business units?

Mark Shafer:

That's a great question, and I'd say a couple of things. I'll begin with the obvious. You need to have a strong math background, the desire to continually learn about applied analytics, and the ability to connect the dots. Then there are the characteristics that are often missed, such as the need to have an entrepreneurial spirit in that you're always looking for new opportunities. Creativity and innovation are central to the Walt Disney Company. I would argue that revenue management/analytics are still in their absolute infancy. Recognizing all those opportunities that are out there and pursuing those should be a passion and a priority.

A piece that will also drive success is storytelling. Many folks are uncomfortable with math or analytics. You have to find ways to build stories around those analytics so that people can better understand the approach and buy in to it. At Disney, we're storytellers. Analytics simply allow us to add numbers to help tell a better story.

Also, individuals that have the skills to identify with the end user of the analytical tools and grasp existing processes will succeed greatly in this business. This is important, as it is one thing to actually develop a software solution that provides the analytics and does a great job of that, but the next piece is what's often missed: the integration of those solutions. You have to understand the business and make sure the solutions integrate appropriately. Say you're working with a team and they've always worked in Excel. Many times we'll develop a software solution that has all the great intelligence behind it, but the front end will look very much like the Excel spreadsheet their team is familiar with, so there's very little process change required of those end users. It's about integrating complex analytics processes with user-friendly business solutions.

The last characteristic I would add is to act like a thermostat. Think of individuals as falling into two buckets: thermometers and thermostats. Your thermometers are going to tell you what's happening, call out opportunities, or potential risks but do very little to act on these opportunities or risks. The thermostats on the other hand are like thermometers and recognize opportunities and potential risks but they also act on these opportunities. That is absolutely critical. Because whether you're evangelizing, developing, or implementing analytics you can be assured you will hit obstacles. You will always run into issues: data issues, buy-in issues, science issues, and integration issues. Therefore, to be successful you have to have that tenacity and the will to succeed to overcome these obstacles. That is the thermostat-type behavior that is a critical characteristic.

Andreas Hinterhuber:

How do you begin to develop an analytical software solution?

Mark Shafer:

When you are looking for an analytic solution, you want to make sure that you don't just limit your search to your own industry. Every industry does something really, really well. What you want to do is identify the best in each of those industries and try to figure out how to leverage those insights. You need a skill set to try to connect those dots – the ability to see something that doesn't look anything like what you're looking for. But if you look with a critical eye, you recognize clearly that there are components from this industry that could actually work and carry it over to your own industry.

When we hire, we look for people with diverse backgrounds. A diversity of teams certainly helps us to approach business problems with varied and unique perspectives.

A great example of using other industries as examples was when we worked with this one airline revenue management vendor and recognized the similarities between hotel and airline business problems. Airlines have origin and destination considerations which is very similar to hotels' length-of-stay considerations.

This is one of the primary reasons our centralized organization at Disney has been successful. We have been able to leverage the knowledge across the segments within the Disney Company to solve some of the most difficult business problems.

Here is a simple example:

We forecast box-office receipts for studios for every movie. Keep in mind every release is a new movie. So how do you forecast something that hasn't happened before? This is a very similar business problem Disney Cruise Line faces every time they open a new itinerary. So we will leverage tactics and learnings from our studios forecasting to the Disney Cruise Line new itinerary forecasting.

Andreas Hinterhuber:

Great comments. You mentioned roadblocks to the implementation of revenue management.

Mark Shafer:

It's pretty much the traditional ones, which would be the buy-in issues, data issues, and integration issues. Also, in many cases, the business problems we are trying to solve have never been solved before, which is why we drive a lot of patents. So you have to figure out the appropriate science approach to solve our unique challenges. These are probably the biggest roadblocks that come to mind.

Andreas Hinterhuber:

You said before: don't be stuck to your own industry. Learn from the very best regardless of where they're coming from. This leads to the next question: from whom are you currently learning?

Mark Shafer:

Well, every industry does something really, really well, and they're all improving. You can't just look at any one industry and say "Oh, that's where you want to go." You've got to look at them all, and just really try to figure out the best of breed from these industries to solve your specific business problem.

And that is what I like about using the *Journal of Revenue and Pricing Management*; leveraging those learnings across industries, whether it's an airline example, or a hotel example, or a supply chain example, whatever the case may be. Whenever something is in there, because it is multi-industry, try to use that and leverage that for your own industry. Just look for the best. But you've got to stay on top of all those industries.

I would also say we do have a big focus on machine learning. We're finding more and more applications. So that's a big investment for us.

Andreas Hinterhuber:

You use artificial intelligence and machine learning to automate processes which are done manually at present?

Mark Shafer:

Yes, or even just an improvement to existing solutions. In some cases we may use statistical models that provide segmentation and forecasting, and in some cases we may move more towards machine learning because it just does a better job. Especially when you've got a lot of data coming in and it's an ever-evolving industry, particularly anything online. It's constantly evolving. If you have, like with machine learning, the ability to adapt and learn and make changes quickly, it certainly helps.

Andreas Hinterhuber:

How do you see the future of revenue management at Walt Disney? One important part clearly is the focus on machine learning and artificial intelligence.

Mark Shafer:

Yes. But the other piece – literally what we're always doing – is going out there and looking for where people are making business decisions. Just simply thinking about all the business decisions that are made in any company, probably thousands if not millions of decisions are made every single day. What we're trying to do is go out and identify some of those where, if we use analytics and decision science, we can drive better business decisions.

We don't limit ourselves to traditional revenue management, as I said before. Literally, we're looking for any place where we can simply drive better business decisions through the application of decision science.

Andreas Hinterhuber:

Great little piece. Evandro, you also had a set of questions.

Evandro Pollono:

Indeed. In the experience of Hinterhuber & Partners you need a theory and a process to implement lasting changes in pricing and, quite frankly, in any other area that affects how people work together in organizations. I will cite the 8-step change model by Kotter (1995) or the Change Acceleration Process by General Electric (Ulrich, Kerr, & Ashkenas, 2002) as examples of such a theory. What theory or process do you use to get buy-in for your initiatives in pricing and revenue management?

Mark Shafer:

We have very clear steps once we've got buy-in to start a process developing an analytics software solution. But before that, we have a lot of conversations. A couple of things we've learned over the years is that simply hearing the successes from us – a central function – is usually not enough. What better way to share success than from a partner who has already seen the benefit of our approach? So, many times we'll make sure that perhaps one key partner of ours will hear a success story from another key partner.

That's the advantage of the conference. Attendees get to hear the learnings from other business segments, not just from us. If you ever came to my office, you'll see that I have hundreds of books. I'm always giving out books. Again, hearing it not just from us but from a third party clearly makes a difference in getting people to buy in to analytics. So if I know of a particular book that has a success story in it, where someone applied analytics in a very similar situation, I'll make sure I give our partner that book.

The other piece is constantly developing everyone's acumen when it comes to analytics. It's a huge component. The conference does just that; it is a forum for education. The best thing I can have is someone across the table from me, a partner of mine who helped develop that analytic solution, to be fully aware and knowledgeable when it comes to analytics. So the more I can get the company to reach that level, the better off we are. One of the key components is not just evangelizing it – we're also developing our customers into very smart analytic leaders. Besides the conference, we send out quarterly newsletters containing success stories and learnings from our various partners within Disney. As you can see, we are all about having multiple touch points for analytics education. But it doesn't stop there.

We also take the best presentations from our conference and present them online regularly throughout the year as part of our Speaker Encore series. So we're constantly exposing our partners with the opportunity of development when it comes to analytics. That development is essential to getting around the barrier of an unfamiliarity with analytics and more specifically what our department does to help drive business results.

Then, when there is an opportunity to pursue a new idea, you're already ahead of the game. So don't start just simply by saying "I found a solution," which you then go out and sell. Start way before that. Get everyone starting to buy in to the value of analytics. Get them to understand the value of data-driven decisions. The value of moving away from averages, to quote Sam Savage and *The Flaw of Averages* (2009). I've probably given out a 100 copies of this book – it's very good, easy to read. Most places start with simply making decisions based on averages, which is not a bad place to start; however if you can just move them away from averages, to understand the distribution around those averages, that's not only a huge science leap, it's also a huge win for the organization and in many cases drives significant value. We are always looking for these types of opportunities: science that improves decision quality that in turn creates value.

Evandro Pollono:

Great insight. The other, fundamental insight is to have a game plan in mind where you start almost like it was a journey and you continuously maintain the organizational energy towards analytics and revenue management.

Mark Shafer:

Absolutely. That's exactly right. It's never a single decision. It literally is a mindset. We always talk about revenue management as a discipline not an application. It's a mindset you have to get started. Like I said, don't wait for the opportunity to actually go ahead and apply analytics somewhere to start evangelizing analytics. Start fostering the mindset in advance of any analytical application.

There are many opportunities you'll never even see that are buried within your organization. I'd say right now, as an example, when we first began doing analytics for the enterprise, I'd say probably 90 percent of the opportunities came from us identifying them. I would say it's almost 50/50 if not 60/40 that now our clients, our partners, are reaching out to us: they are now identifying the opportunities. They have been able to identify them because they've developed their own framework on analytics and the discipline for how to think about their business, with our help of course. Self-realization is what continues to evolve.

Andreas Hinterhuber:

In summary: at the beginning, 90 percent of the opportunities in revenue management were identified at a central level, whereas now about 60 percent of opportunities are generated at a decentralized level by your own partners.

Mark Shafer:

That's exactly right. What's exciting is that opportunities are now generated by all of the segments and all departments across the Walt Disney Company. Analytics can solve the wide array of business problems in every discipline. So you have to make sure you bring this discipline across the organization and there are lots of unique ways that analytics are implemented across our company.

I think many people start out with something simple like "I wanted to implement revenue management." Then they try to start evangelizing revenue management. But they should start even before that. Start evangelizing analytics, data-driven decisions, decision science, to everyone in advance, and all those various opportunities will start to unveil themselves. As I have mentioned, buy-in is always the greatest challenge so the earlier you can start promoting Evangalytics®, the better!

Evandro Pollono:

Great insight, very well said. I would like to explore one further point. You say you encourage people to bring new ideas from other industries. How do you decide which ideas to implement? Let's say you have ten people with ten ideas. How do you say, "Okay, we're going with this one, run some experiments, but we will drop the other nine"?

Mark Shafer:

That's a very good question, Evandro. When we prioritize our workload – and we have to because, as you can imagine, I could be doing this for another hundred years and I wouldn't be able to catch up with everything that's still out there – we do a couple of things.

One obvious thing is to identify the highest value. Value could be defined as anything from enhancing the overall guest experience to improving profitability. Different projects have different definitions of value. The other things we certainly look for are speed to market. Also, how clean is the data? Has the data ever been used in this way before? The buy-in is huge. Is the opportunity being identified by the end client, or is it coming from us? If it's coming from the end client, that means there's a lot more buy-in typically. So we certainly prefer opportunities coming from decentralized units.

Lastly, I would say is take into account the ability to leverage components or learnings from one business problem to another. This in itself assists my earlier comment on the importance of speed to market. We have developed many really good solutions that we frequently leverage across our projects. When we see success with a solution, this makes the buy-in from our partners much easier to achieve.

Evandro Pollono:

Mark, are there any further points that we should explore in the area of implementing pricing and revenue management?

Mark Shafer:

There are a couple of things I want to make sure we call out. Many times when we think about applying analytics or applying revenue management, we think of it as a go or no-go decision. We tend to think the initiative has an investment profile. We tend to think about the value the initiative is going to bring. But the piece, I think, that's often missed is not only the potential expansion in revenues, but the *effect on the organization if you do not pursue analytics*. That is key: your competition does something like revenue management and you don't. Or your competition is smarter about movie selection or forecasting than you are – what are the implications of that? If I say that I will not pursue this opportunity today, I will do it in the future based on capital constraints, what are the potential financial repercussions of not acting? Recognize that you're not simply forgoing revenues, you may be forgoing your existing base, if you will. That's something you have to be very careful with.

I would argue today we're very much in a global analytics race. You have to recognize that yesterday's strategies, strategic advantage, can quickly become tomorrow's industry standard. So there's a cost to doing nothing. I think that's a piece we often miss.

Andreas Hinterhuber:

Mark, I will quote you on this one: the cost of doing nothing is not zero. This is a great, quotable quote.

Mark Shafer:

Thank you. The other piece I would also remind everyone about is that you're never done. Take our hotel revenue management model. We implemented hotel revenue management 21 years ago, and we're constantly improving it. Even though it is perhaps one of our more sophisticated solutions, we're not done. We are constantly evolving the solution: the science is getting better, the processing power allows us to do more, and the business environment is changing. You have to recognize that you're forever evolving. You are never done. There's a quote by Walt Disney that I like to use a lot: "Let your past inspire you. Let it motivate you. But never let it hold you back." It's something we think about a lot around here. We are always looking for ways to improve.

Andreas Hinterhuber:

Great. Mark, I really appreciate your insight on the cost of doing nothing. Essentially you suggest: elevate the cost of doing nothing to energize the entire organization to act.

Mark Shafer:

Exactly. One last piece, and I will finish here with this, is to recognize your system biases as well as your data biases. Be very transparent about those to the end user so they know how to interpret the results or recommendations. That is absolutely critical. We have a saying here: "All our solutions are tools, not rules." You still have to make sure that there is oversight in all these solutions. Our people are still very important to the success of our solutions. The key point is be conscientious and transparent about the biases of the solution and the data. There are always biases, and you have to interpret the results appropriately. Educate your people and promote Evangalytics® in your organization in order to achieve maximum business success.

Andreas Hinterhuber:

I would agree with you on this one. Biases are real and pervasive and I, too, study them passionately (Hinterhuber, 2015).

Mark, we really enjoyed our conversation. Thank you for your time and insights and for the privilege of this firsthand intellectual exchange on a fascinating topic.

Evandro Pollono:

Thank you; we really enjoyed this exchange of ideas.

Mark Shafer:

Thank you for this opportunity.

Acknowledgments

Reprinted with permission from Hinterhuber, A., Pollono, E., & Shafer, M. (2018), Elevating the cost of doing nothing: an interview with Mark Shafer, *Journal of Revenue and Pricing Management*, 17 (1), 3–10. All rights reserved: Copyright Macmillan Publishers Ltd., part of Springer Nature, 2017.

References

Healy, P. 2014. Ticket Pricing Puts 'Lion King' Atop Broadway's Circle of Life. *New York Times*, A1.

Hinterhuber, A. 2015. Violations of Rational Choice Principles in Pricing Decisions. *Industrial Marketing Management*, 47: 65–74.

Hinterhuber, A., and S. M. Liozu. 2017. The Micro-Foundations of Pricing. *Journal of Business Research*, 76: 159–162.

Kotter, J. P. 1995. Leading Change: Why Transformation Efforts Fail. *Harvard Business Review*, 73 (2): 59–67.

Savage, S. L. 2009. *The Flaw of Averages: Why We Underestimate Risk in the Face of Uncertainty*. Hoboken, NJ: Wiley.

Ulrich, D., S. Kerr, and R. Ashkenas. 2002. *The GE Work-Out: How to Implement GE's Revolutionary Method for Busting Bureaucracy and Attacking Organizational Problems – Fast!* New York: McGraw-Hill.

Part 3
Pricing strategy implementation
The role of the sales force

4 The role of the sales force in pricing strategy implementation

Andreas Hinterhuber and Frank Cespedes

> This interview discusses the critical role of the sales force in pricing strategy implementation. Among the critical skills that effective business-to-business (B2B) sales managers must master are value quantification capabilities.

Andreas Hinterhuber:

What are the key capabilities for the sales manager and the strategic account manager (SAM) in the future versus today?

Frank Cespedes:

Selling, sales management, and account management requirements are changing – quickly and with implications for other functions and activities in companies – but *not* in ways typically discussed in the business press and many popular sales books.

For example, it is not true that salespeople are being "disintermediated" or replaced by online interactions. In the US, the internet has been a fact for nearly 30 years. Yet, according to the US Bureau of Labor Statistics (BLS), the number of salespeople in the US has *increased* in the 21st century to more than 10 percent of the labor force.[1] Further, the BLS data almost certainly undercount the reality because, in increasingly service economies like those in the US, Europe, and other places, business developers are often called associates, managing directors, or vice presidents, not placed in a "sales" category for labor-department reporting purposes. But selling is what they do.

Similarly, e-commerce has been there since the introduction of the internet. Yet, after decades, about 12 percent of total retail sales in the US in 2017 were online sales. That figure includes Amazon, and almost half the non-Amazon portion of e-commerce is via the online sites of brick-and-mortar retailers. Even if this online percentage doubles or triples in the next decade (and that is unlikely because the growth rate of online sales has been decreasing in the past five years), the majority of retail sales is still done in stores.

US companies spend, annually, on their sales efforts more than three times what they spend on all their media advertising, and more than ten times what they spend on social media and all other digital marketing initiatives. Selling expenses and the sales force are, by far, the biggest and most expensive part of strategy execution for most firms.

What *is* changing is the nature of sales tasks. Consider the process of buying a car. Consumers do a lot of online research: the average US car shopper now spends over 11 hours online and only about 3.5 hours offline in trips to dealerships during their buying journeys. But the vast majority of consumers still purchase their cars in person at a dealer. Further, research indicates that their online sources of information have made consumers place *more* emphasis on their interactions at the dealer with salespeople. However, because buyers can access prices, reviews, and other information via online searches, their attitudes toward negotiations, list prices, and sales behavior at dealers are changing. Smartphones, market forums, and other factors are causing similar changes across many other industries, both B2B and B2C (business-to-consumer).[2]

The most important thing about selling is the buyer. Changes in buying behavior are affecting the capabilities needed by sales managers and SAMs. Rather than moving sequentially through a funnel, buyers (like auto shoppers) now typically engage in parallel activity streams throughout their buying journey. Understanding where prospects and customers are, how they move between streams, and how to interact with them in a given stream is now central to effective selling, sales management, and the implementation of a pricing strategy.

Andreas Hinterhuber:

I would tend to agree: changes in buyer expectations require a change in sales manager capabilities. Value quantification capabilities may be an example. More on this later. For now, let us explore pricing in the context of sales managers. What is your experience in delegating pricing authority to sales/SAMs? Under which circumstances would you expand/restrict pricing authority?

Frank Cespedes:

Where pricing authority resides depends a lot upon context and the buying process. But let's first consider a prerequisite for even considering delegation of pricing authority to sales: having in place a relevant and coherent sales compensation plan.

Compensation is perhaps the most discussed aspect of sales management – even though research indicates that coaching, reviews, and other performance-management practices typically have more impact on actual selling behaviors. Surveys consistently indicate that, across industries, about 65 to 75 percent of firms set sales incentives on the basis of volume – that is, on how much is sold irrespective of the price, margin, or cost to serve customers.

In an incentive plan like that, the message to salespeople is "sell to anyone because there is no such thing as a 'bad' customer"; and reps will, rationally, discount price to make the sale and make quota. This misalignment is not hard to understand intellectually. But many companies still do this. As a result, industries are filled with companies that get what they pay for (e.g., salespeople who, responding to their volume-driven incentives, fail to execute a premium-priced strategy) and don't get what they don't pay for (e.g., individually focused incentives for SAMs who must work with others in a team-selling approach to key, multi-location accounts). So the first step in potentially delegating pricing authority is to make sure your sales-incentive plan encourages the behavior you need.

Second, it's important to distinguish between a price and pricing. Competition, supply and demand, other market factors, and – by voting with their feet – customers ultimately determine what they will pay in terms of price. In a given context, salespeople may or may not possess the best local knowledge to help negotiate that price with specific customers. But it's the selling company's responsibility to set pricing – that is, the structure of prices for a given product–service configuration. A price is not the same thing as pricing. Customers ultimately determine price. But you and your organization do pricing, including the framing and delivery of the value proposition. Then, whether salespeople should have significant pricing authority or not depends, in my view, more on buying processes than on product type. There are successful and unsuccessful examples of centralized and decentralized pricing in both commodity and specialty product categories. The more relevant variables are who buys and how, not what they buy.

Historically, many firms delegated price authority to individual salespeople because the time required for sales to get pricing approval from headquarters, their managers, or a centralized pricing office was long and cumbersome. Technology is fast overcoming that constraint. But any process – including pricing – is only as good as the people who manage that process.

Andreas Hinterhuber:

Can you give us some examples of best-in-class companies from industry in pricing strategy implementation?

Frank Cespedes:

Best practices in pricing vary by type of business, stage of business, and competitive context. Market forces can soon make today's example of "best in class" tomorrow's case study about marketing myopia. That said, I would cite as long-term good examples of pricing implementation Apple for tangible tech products, Disney in B2C, Paccar in B2B, Louis Vuitton in luxury goods, and some software-as-a-service (SaaS) firms about whom I teach case studies in my courses at Harvard Business School.

In my experience, however, a key issue in effective pricing implementation is understanding the role and goal of price in your particular business model. The role of price, and therefore what constitutes best practice in price implementation, varies significantly depending upon, for example, whether the company is involved in project pricing, product pricing, the pricing of a product–service package, or seeking an early-mover advantage where (in theory at least) we initially sell low with profitable monetization coming later by upselling the installed base.

These are very different pricing roles and, as always, the specific buying-behavior context is crucial. Consider, for example, consumer internet companies and the currently fashionable "freemium" pricing approach. The common business model here is a two-sided platform with a chicken-and-egg dynamic: you must attract users in order to attract consumers or firms willing to use your site and pay to advertise on your site. Hence, to sign up users and build that part of the platform, initial "free" pricing to consumers is common.

This sounds plausible because there's typically almost no or very low marginal costs to digital goods. So the plan is to acquire users with free services until inertia or switching costs kick in, and then you charge for additional capacity, extras, or premium features. It seems to have worked beautifully for companies like Dropbox, LinkedIn, and Skype. But so many other freemium-pricing companies have basically enacted the old joke about selling each pencil below cost while hoping to make it up in volume. Why?

Usually, only 1 to 2 percent of users will upgrade to a paid product. Therefore, the size of the target market counts in adopting this pricing approach. A choice of features for free and the managing of a built-in tension are important implementation issues in this approach: offer too many features, and there's no incentive to upgrade (the plague of most current SaaS businesses); offer too few, and you cannot generate enough initial users to make your site attractive to advertisers or others on the other side of the platform. The product–customer context matters. Note the dynamics of services like Atlassian or Basecamp (collaborative software), Dropbox (cloud sharing files), LinkedIn, and Skype: in part, you sign up for and use these services because other important people in your life (colleagues, prospective employers, friends, family) use them. The presence or absence of peer pressure and social switching costs is often the foundation for the success of this pricing approach.

Therefore, my counsel to executives is always to be wary of trying to use someone else's "secret sauce" in the recipe of their business model. Best practice is what works here, not there.

Andreas Hinterhuber:

Let us explore the idea of excellence in pricing strategy implementation. How should companies begin this journey?

Frank Cespedes:

"Journey" is the right word because, in a competitive market, effective pricing is a process, not a one-and-done analytical study of willingness-to-pay. The journey begins with identifying customer value, and it requires ongoing price testing to make sure we are still traveling in the right direction as market conditions inevitably change.

In my MBA and executive courses, I often assign a note about pricing which (among other things) discusses a company called Zolam (disguised name). Zolam is a chemical firm serving diverse global markets characterized at the time by declining demand, industry over-capacity, and capital market pressures to increase earnings. Not a happy situation. Zolam initially responded by stressing new technology complemented by product-line cuts, reduced inventory and service levels, and other cost-cutting moves. But these moves did not appreciably improve earnings. Zolam's leadership eventually focused on pricing as a way to win profitable business.

Zolam's leaders began with a consistent message, "We must understand what is valuable in order to be valuable." In meetings across functions, they repeatedly asked how specific products, services, or other benefits impacted customers including, but not limited to, their customers' financial success. Buying decisions always have at least two dimensions: the benefits that customers value, and how they buy. Zolam's customers included firms that package pharmaceuticals and to whom it sold rubber stoppers used to cap injectable drugs – a product long viewed as a low-price "commodity." But Zolam found a hierarchy of benefits in this simple product.

The base level was to minimize customer acquisition costs of the stopper. The next level was to reduce possession and usage costs through design and delivery initiatives that increased customers' packaging-line speeds, lowered their inventory requirements, and aided their manufacturing-capacity planning. A third level was to help customers increase *their* product's performance. Zolam found, for instance, that stoppers molded in unique colors helped hospitals and doctors reduce errors and lower insurance costs, yielding a higher price for Zolam's packaging customers and less churn in their customer base.

Adopting this value-based approach across its product line, Zolam developed metrics, customer profiles, and new account-review processes for its salespeople. Different customers, or the same customer at different times, had different purchasing criteria and price elasticities, depending upon the usage application. This approach and the consequent data and testing allowed Zolam to clarify target price, reservation price, and the price-negotiation strategy relevant in a given buying context. In turn, salespeople were trained and incentivized in line with this approach, which generally meant calling on different people at different organizational levels within their assigned accounts.

Then, you must credibly communicate the value being delivered. Zolam did this through frequent reviews, after the sale, with key people at targeted accounts. In many other businesses, however, it's important to find ways of doing this before the sale. A good example is Paccar, maker of Kenworth and Peterbilt trucks, which Paccar sells for about a 20 percent price premium versus its competitors. Paccar salespeople qualify customers with an online interactive detailing of expenses incurred during the life of a truck, with data supplied by the prospect. You can input gasoline costs, tire-rolling coefficients, and vehicle weights to quantify the benefits of a Paccar truck versus lower-priced alternatives. You can do the same for resale value, maintenance, driver retention (useful data if you run a fleet), and financing costs. The firm's website also provides a fuel-economy primer aptly titled "Push Less Air, Pull More Profit."

Andreas Hinterhuber:

Let's get down to the individual sales manager. What are, in your view, characteristics – personality traits – of sales managers who excel in pricing strategy implementation? What are, by contrast, personality traits or behavioral characteristics that make the individual sales or strategic account manager less effective?

Frank Cespedes:

Popular sales methodology books, and many sales training firms, focus on personality traits. However, most of these assessments read like a horoscope ("can listen but challenge") or like a bland summary of traits such as "modesty, conscientiousness, curiosity, an achievement orientation, lack of discouragement" and so on. At best, these lists of personality traits remind us that people tend to do business with people they like, or that certain basics of human interactions (listen, don't interrupt, make sure you understand the other person's perspective, etc.) are relevant in most sales contexts.

But the search for personality traits in effective selling, including pricing implementation, is fundamentally flawed. Research about the links between personality traits and selling effectiveness has been conducted for nearly a century. The results are inconsistent and, in most cases, contradictory and not replicable – that is, study X asserts a positive correlation between certain personality traits and sales performance, and study Y finds in a different context a negative correlation.

These inconsistent results tell us something significant: so much depends on the buying situation, that what academic researchers call a "contingency approach" is necessary. More simply stated, the research suggests that certain common stereotypes of a "good" salesperson (e.g., pleasing personality, deep inventory of stories, hard-wired for sociability, and so on) are indeed just stereotypes. Sales talent – and sales failure – comes in all shapes and sizes. No one size fits all.

Here is how I think of the traits and characteristics relevant to sales and pricing effectiveness. First, recognize that multiple factors cause sales, including – but not limited to – price, the skills of the salesperson, and the quality and relevance of the product being sold at a given price. Another important factor is customer selection, or what the strategy literature calls the "scope" of the business – in other words, decisions that companies are always making, implicitly or explicitly, about where they do and do not focus in a market (see Figure 4.1).

Second, understand the key sales tasks in that business (see Figure 4.2). To do this, always begin with the externals in your business, not internal price lists. Value in any business is created or destroyed in the marketplace with customers, not in conference rooms or research studies. Key externals include the industry you compete in, the market and product segments where you choose to play, and the nature of the buying criteria at the customers you target. These factors determine the required sales tasks – that is, what your go-to-market initiatives must accomplish to deliver and extract value via your

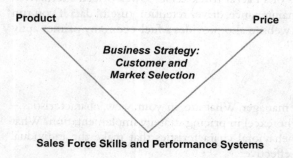

Figure 4.1 What causes sales? A combination of factors.

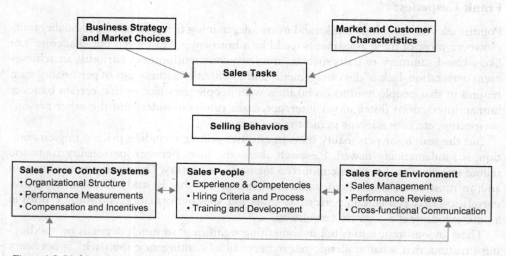

Figure 4.2 Linking strategy and sales.

(*Source*: F. Cespedes, *Aligning Strategy and Sales*, Harvard Business Review Press, 2014)

pricing approach, and therefore what your salespeople must be good at to implement your approach effectively.

Then, the issue is aligning actual selling behaviors (including pricing) with the required sales tasks and using the appropriate levers for doing that. The key levers in most businesses are displayed along the bottom of Figure 4.2:

- Salespeople: who they are, what they know, how you hire and then develop their skills and attitudes over time, so that they are good at executing your firm's required sales tasks, not those of a generic selling methodology or what they learned at another company that made a different set of strategic and pricing choices.
- Sales control systems: the systems that shape ongoing performance-management practices, including how the sales force is organized, key performance indicators (e.g., volume? margin? profit-per-sale? other?) used to measure sales effectiveness, and sales compensation and incentive systems.
- Sales force environment: the wider organizational environment in which pricing and other go-to-market initiatives are developed and executed; how communication does or doesn't work across organizational boundaries (e.g., between product and sales groups in the firm); how sales managers are selected and developed; the conduct of performance reviews.

Selling effectiveness is not a generalized trait. It's a function of the specific sales tasks. Therefore, the relevant personality is the personality, and skills, relevant for those tasks in that market for that selling company.

I believe the same is true when it comes to personality and pricing. In a transactions-intensive, inside sales model where the pricing is part of a land-and-expand sales approach with accounts, you almost certainly want a different type of customer-contact person than you do in a longer-selling-cycle, product-service solutions model where upfront pricing requires effective framing and articulation of a more complex value proposition. My view is that managers should begin with understanding the relevant sales tasks, not an elusive search for a set of all-purpose personality traits.

Andreas Hinterhuber:

What other pieces of advice do you have for companies that struggle in getting pricing/value creation strategies implemented?

Frank Cespedes:

Based on my experience with companies, I'll offer three final pieces of advice.

"Everyone else does it this way." Avoid this mindset. Pricing is a visible moment-of-truth in business, and many managers take refuge in the herd – that is, "established" industry practice. But the essence of strategy is being smart about being different. Pricing is where you test the coherence of a business strategy and value proposition. Herd pricing also runs the risk that prices are the legacy of obsolete market circumstances and sales tasks in that industry.

Cost-based pricing is easier to explain. Evidence supports this intuition. Behavioral researchers have charted a phenomenon across countries, cultures, and economic systems: people in Communist countries reacted to various cost-based pricing scenarios in ways not very different than people in Beverly Hills. But when you *are* providing differentiated value, the issue is framing price appropriately. At the gas pump, the credit price is typically the default price, while paying by cash garners a "discount." Over a century ago, Marshall Field pioneered the concept of the retail bargain basement. As a place for slow-moving or out-of-fashion goods from upstairs, the basement helped keep higher-margin offerings on the main levels and, by relegating specific products downstairs, buyers from each department freed up shelf space for faster-turning items. Customers did not object; they bought. Few customers wake up in the morning wanting to pay a higher price. But most seek value.

Price testing. Price is a dynamic variable in any business, affected by changes over the product life cycle or as a company seeks to move from early adopters to more mainstream customer segments. Hence, testing prices as buyers and buying behavior changes is crucial. But relatively few companies do that. Or, they rely primarily on surveys, and there are systematic differences between how people respond to surveys and their actual behavior in the marketplace.

Admittedly, testing price in a business context presents challenges that are qualitatively different from the circumstances surrounding academic market research or clinical trials. There are relatively few opportunities for randomized controlled experiments in a changing, competitive market. But increased access to data, new technologies for A/B tests, the ability to change prices online, or to run online ads with different prices at different times, are all making price testing more accessible. There is less excuse not to test prices on an ongoing basis. As usual in business, the real constraint is managerial.

Andreas Hinterhuber:

Frank, thank you for sharing your insights.

Frank Cespedes teaches at Harvard Business School. He ran a professional services firm for 12 years, has consulted with companies in many industries, and has been a board member of startup firms, established companies, and private equity organizations. He has written for numerous publications and is the author of six books including, most recently, *Aligning Strategy and Sales: The Choices, Systems, and Behaviors That Drive Effective Selling* (Harvard Business Review Press), which was cited as "the best sales book of the year" (*Strategy & Business*), "a must read" (*Gartner*), and "perhaps the best sales book ever" (*Forbes*).

Notes

1 See the BLS website for sales employment: www.bls.gov/oes/current/oes410000.htm.
2 For data about auto buying, see F.V. Cespedes and J. Hamilton, "Selling to Customers Who Do Their Homework Online," *Harvard Business Review* (HBR.org, 16 March 2016). For data about buying and sales interactions across a variety of other industries, see F.V. Cespedes and T. Bova, "What Salespeople Need to Know about the New B2B Landscape," *Harvard Business Review* (HBR.org, 5 August 2015).

5 The strategic account manager as ecosystem captain
Driving profits via pricing

Andreas Hinterhuber and Bernard Quancard

> This interview discusses the changing role of the strategic account manager (SAM). SAMs, in the future, will be ecosystem captains capable of managing complex relationships and teams, organizing data, and telling stories with analytics. SAMs in the future will be assessed along a set of metrics that are similar to metrics of how top management consultants are evaluated: activities, competencies, intermediary results, quantified business impact with customers, and short-term business development targets.

Andreas Hinterhuber:

The focus of our discussion is the implementation of pricing strategies and, more generally, of commercial excellence programs. We find that companies that manage pricing well concentrate on several critical dimensions: price setting, price getting, the organizational infrastructure, analytics, organizational capabilities, and incentive systems. In the absence of further data, these points are usually critical levers that executives can and should activate to drive profits via pricing. Exploring these – and potentially many other – levers is the topic of our book.

Bernard Quancard:

Well said. I would agree.

Andreas Hinterhuber:

Let's begin with the role of the account manager and pricing: what are the trends in pricing in the context of strategic account management?

Bernard Quancard:

The role of the strategic account manager is changing, and we, SAMA, the Strategic Account Management Association, have changed our mission statement to reflect this change.

The big change is this: it is not enough to manage customer–supplier relationships – suppliers must manage the entire ecosystem of their customers. Managing ecosystems allows for value creation and value capture. For example, if you're building an automation system for a GM plant in China, you're going to deal with machine tool manufacturers in Germany, you might have to deal with an engineering company in Italy, and maybe an installer company in Singapore. You now have an ecosystem that contributes to value creation for the final customer. So, the big change is that the strategic account manager, the SAM, is an ecosystem captain. He or she is no longer driving customer–supplier relationships. That's a big change.

Becoming an ecosystem captain requires a dramatically new set of competencies: the ability to manage a multidisciplinary, complex team is one. The ability to organize data is another important capability. Data tell stories, so the SAM becomes an analytical storyteller.

The profile of the SAM in this respect is similar to that of a McKinsey, BCG, or other top management consultant. This is the profile towards which the SAM is evolving, driven by abundance of data and by the need to manage the customer ecosystem.

Andreas Hinterhuber:

The best consultants are thought leaders. The best consultants can help clients evolve toward a future that the clients do not fully understand but that the consultants, thanks to their domain-specific competencies, experience, and relationships, are able to envision. The fundamental idea is that consultants and clients co-create a vision for the future and the roadmap to get there. There is one business leader who expressed this thought superbly well: Pascal Kemps, then vice president with DHL, today head of pricing with Securitas, in our previous book emphasized that SAMs should position themselves as the best possible partners to help clients evolve toward a weakly defined future (Hinterhuber and Kemps 2017).

In summary: my strong conviction is that consultants have to be thought leaders; your take is that the SAM is evolving also towards the role of consultant.

Bernard Quancard:

Yes, and the key is that I am going to co-create with you value which will impact your business model and your business outcomes. So, it's all about customer business outcomes and the customer business model. I don't even look at my product anymore. I'm selling solutions or ideas which impact your business outcomes, whether it's growth, profitability, innovation, or customer satisfaction. I'm selling business outcomes. That's the key.

Andreas Hinterhuber:

Very well said.

Bernard Quancard:

So, I have to know the industry of the customer better than they do, and I have to know the business model of the customer better than they do, because I want to quantify for them the impact of my solution for their business outcomes.

Andreas Hinterhuber:

It all comes down to the value quantification capability: it's all about quantifying business outcomes.

Bernard Quancard:

That's exactly the point. Price is a natural consequence of co-value creation: pricing may take many forms, from simple to complex models, but the point is that price is a consequence of co-value creation.

Andreas Hinterhuber:

Value first, then price. On this, I think, we agree. Which company is, in your view, a possible best-practice example in the area of value quantification and pricing? I'm aware that, first of all, practices change: what's good today may be irrelevant tomorrow. Second, by singling out a particular company there is a risk that those who are not singled out are perceived as less good, which is not necessarily the case. But again, there are individuals associated with particular companies that are associated with traits of excellence.

Bernard Quancard:

There are senior managers in pricing, account management, and marketing at DHL, Schneider Electric, HP, and IBM, to name a few, who have achieved excellence in pricing, value co-creation, and implementing the pricing decisions.

Andreas Hinterhuber:

Let's talk about SAM and pricing. We first need to keep in mind the very clear division of labor between sales and strategic account management. We also need to keep in mind that the sales function typically has pricing authority. What's the role of the strategic account management function in pricing?

Bernard Quancard:

We recently conducted a research project with the University of Mannheim which suggested the existence of four different go-to-market models in the context of strategic account management. These different models have differing implications also for pricing.

One: purely transactional relationships for, for example, commodity products. Here the SAM has no role in pricing. Two: highly competitive markets with shortlisted suppliers: Again, in that situation the SAM has a very limited role in pricing. Three: solutions with a high degree of standardization. Take Schneider Electric and its energy management system, which is fairly standardized. In that case the SAM has a consultative role in pricing: pricing is driven by dedicated pricing teams or, in their absence, by marketing or finance. But here the SAM is expected to contribute. Four: trusted advisor relationships where value is co-created. Here, the SAM has the pricing lead.

In sum: four models, from purely transactional relationships (no role for the SAM) to shortlisted suppliers (a very limited role for the SAM) to standard solutions (a consultative role for the SAM) to, finally, trusted advisor relationships (SAMs drive pricing). This is my view.

Andreas Hinterhuber:

In sum: the logic of value creation influences the organization of pricing. And this in turn influences a fundamentally important tool in pricing implementation: the account pricing plan. For commodity products the account pricing plan is largely driven by sales managers. For shortlisted suppliers it is most likely the product manager, for standard solutions it could be marketing with input from the SAM, and for trusted advisor relationships the SAM builds the account pricing plan.

Bernard Quancard:

Fantastic comment. The really interesting deals for the SAM in terms of pricing are solutions and trusted advisor relationships. But don't forget that you can be pressured on price also for your solutions if your solution is not very differentiated. Again to energy management, where you could have a Schneider solution competing against Johnson Controls, Siemens, GE, or Eaton. When there is a lot of price pressure, I don't think the SAM or the sales function should have significant pricing responsibility. In these cases you should have a strong input from finance in order to manage prices, costs, and margins well.

Andreas Hinterhuber:

On this point I'm not sure that I'd agree 100 percent. But to your point: you suggest that pricing is a key responsibility of the SAM for customized solutions and for trusted advisor relationships. What's your advice for organizations that want to drive profitability via pricing?

Bernard Quancard:

This is a good question, and this is why we need this book. There is a fundamental difference between the elaboration and the implementation of a pricing strategy. And in the future the SAM must be able to access a key capability – the pricing capability – in the core team. That pricing capability can come from pricing, marketing, product management, or finance. The SAM typically is not able to master the details but needs to have access to dedicated resources that have pricing capabilities.

Take Zurich: for some large, strategic accounts, Zurich has been able to quantify and optimize the total value of the customer risk. Across any large account you could have hundreds of different insurance plans/products for different customer entities, each with a different risk profile. Zurich can go to its customers and make the case that the company is able to save them, say, US$2 million, by optimizing the hundreds of different insurance plans across all the entities of the company. Customers cannot do this by themselves. There will inevitably be many different ways to share the value created, via fees for supplementary services, adjustments to insurance premiums, or a performance bonus. But this discussion is highly technical, and I don't know if the SAM has, or should have, these capabilities. In sum: for customized solutions or trusted advisor relationships, I strongly believe that there should be a pricing competency within the core team.

Andreas Hinterhuber:

I'll summarize what we've discussed and learned from each other. There are products or services where both the supplier and the customer are heavily involved in delivering the final product – customized solutions or collaborative relationships where value is co-created. In these cases, the demands on the SAM are extraordinarily high.

The SAM needs skills in the following domains: analytic capabilities to make sense of big data, storytelling abilities to map out a vision, consulting capabilities to provide unbiased advice, value chain orchestration capabilities to influence the customer's ecosystem, and value quantification capabilities to make the business case. There's a risk, as you suggest, that we overload the role of the SAM if we demand excellence also in pricing. So your take is that for pricing capabilities – and I have to be clear here, not for value quantification capabilities – the SAM should be able to access capabilities from other functions: pricing, finance, or marketing.

Put differently: when it comes down to proposing specific value capture models, when it comes down to proposing specific pricing models, it could very well be that this competency comes from the members of the core team, not from the SAM themselves.

Bernard Quancard:

I completely agree with that.

Andreas Hinterhuber:

The SAM drives value quantification. Specific pricing models are proposed by the SAM, but they can actually originate from other functions.

Bernard Quancard:

Yes. And to your favorite motto "value first, then price" I would add: start with value co-creation, then value quantification and then price. It is co-creation of value, value quantification, and price: price is the consequence of sharing quantified, co-created value.

Andreas Hinterhuber:

Great. What's your advice for companies that recognize the potential for creating value through strategic account management via value quantification and pricing? Where should they start? To guide your thoughts, I add an observation: a deficit I see in companies large and small is that the SAM is basically a rebranded sales manager. This means that, first of all, many companies need a much sharper distinction between the role of the SAM and the role of the sales manager.

Bernard Quancard:

Absolutely. It's a bad choice to rebrand a sales manager as a SAM. The sales manager is a lone wolf; the SAM is an ecosystem captain. The sales manager is not a good listener; the SAM is a consultant. The sales manager closes deals; the SAM is a strategist, a data organizer, and a guardian of long-term relationships.

Andreas Hinterhuber:

Companies thus should define exclusive domains: responsibilities that are exclusive to the sales manager, responsibilities that are exclusive to the SAM, and then an area where the sales manager and the SAM work together.

Bernard Quancard:

Indeed. Developing a strategic account management function with impact requires creating a model of the key traits and competencies necessary for the SAM of the future. Companies should then create an objective pool of talent and gradually move this talent pool into key account management roles. I stress *gradually*: it's important not to disrupt critical customer relationships.

I will refer to Schneider Electric: the company changed 60 percent of their strategic account executives in 2 years. Sixty percent! At least half these executives were recruited externally, from industry but also to a fair degree from consulting companies.

Andreas Hinterhuber:

You begin with a pool of high-caliber SAMs who share the vision of acting as ecosystem captains and as co-creators of value, and you gradually move these SAMs into influential positions.

Bernard Quancard:

Yes, you create a pool; you can test and develop the SAMs with smaller or younger strategic accounts first, and then you gradually manage the transformation process.

Andreas Hinterhuber:

Great. I'd like to get your insight on how to measure and, lest we forget, incentivize the SAM. There is, I think, agreement that roles that aim for a longer-term impact have less emphasis on short-term results and more emphasis on individual activities, competencies, or intermediary results. I'll mention a few examples: short-term results are sales targets which are less useful for the SAM; individual activities could be the number of quantified business cases developed; competencies could be critical skills in big data or consultative selling; and intermediary results could be client feedback or customer engagement/satisfaction scores. This is, I think, fairly well established. So an initial recommendation quite likely takes the following form: the variable incentive for the SAM should be based less on short-term results and more on individual activities, competencies, and intermediary results. But getting the balance right is not easy.

Bernard Quancard:

It's not easy. Best-in-class companies measure business outcomes: growth rates of strategic customers, the amount of business gained without bidding processes, gross margin evolution over time, net promoter scores, and, as I said before, quantified business outcomes (how much money did my customer earn in the given year because of my solutions or because of the value jointly created?). But don't forget that for mature relationships you can and should measure also short-term results. So you put it quite well, and I would expand that you can measure five items: activities, competencies, intermediary results, sales/gross margins, and the amount of quantified business value that the SAM has created.

Andreas Hinterhuber:

That's a great comment. You suggest rewarding the SAM almost identically to how we reward consultants. We also look at consultants' activities; competencies, intermediary results, and – and this is really my passion – quantified business impact with customers. We also measure short-term business development targets. The bottom line is the SAM is increasingly morphing into the role of consultant or trusted advisor and therefore should be rewarded as such.

Bernard Quancard:

That's a great insight.

Andreas Hinterhuber:

Let's get down to behavioral and psychological traits of the SAM. How would you characterize the SAM of the future?

Bernard Quancard:

Three things come up. One: the ability to characterize a problem, so that characterizing the problem will lead to significant co-value creation. In the case of Zurich, the ability to characterize a problem is related not to mapping products to customers or analyzing product gross margins but to understanding the total cost of risk that the customer is carrying and to insights into how to optimize the total cost of risk with good margins for the supplier. So a good SAM with the perspective of an outsider has these diagnostic skills: the mindset, the attitude, the strategic thinking ability, the ability to identify problems – these are very important.

Two: value innovation. You have to be a value innovator: you take data and generate novel insights with this data. So you and your team generate insights from customer data that allow you to create new value.

Three: you have to be a transformation agent. The co-creation of value transforms customers, and the transformation process is not so easy. You have to be a good leader, you have to convince, you have to reassure people that they need to take the risk, you have to be a good transformation agent.

Andreas Hinterhuber:

You emphasize three vital traits: the ability to identify a problem, the ability to generate novel insights with data, and the ability to transform organizations. The first trait you mentioned is about pattern recognition: A great SAM, you say, will recognize a pattern and be able to come up with a proposal that the average SAM will miss. Pascal Kemps, now head of pricing at Securitas – we mentioned him already – shared the following experience (Hinterhuber and Kemps 2017). A large account published a request for proposal for a given freight volume. Pascal and his team, then at DHL, demonstrated to the customer that this volume was too high and proposed a solution that ended up reducing the sales volume for DHL: "That's a sacrifice you have to make" (Hinterhuber and Kemps 2017: 164), says

Kemps, but the fundamental point is that DHL positions itself as a true consultant acting in the customer's best interest, even if doing so reduces sales volume for DHL as supplier. It's clear, you'll agree, that this has a dramatic impact on the quality of the relationship with the customer. I encourage you to read the full story.

Bernard Quancard:

Great comment. I will.

Andreas Hinterhuber:

The next question is about the procurement process. You mentioned that one indicator of the performance of the SAM is the amount of business won without a bid. Fair point. This requires that SAMs change the purchase decision criteria or, more so, how procurement is done. Any insights?

Bernard Quancard:

My first advice: try to understand the present dashboard of procurement. Some SAMs have no idea – I repeat, no idea – about the dashboard of procurement!

Andreas Hinterhuber:

I tend to agree.

Bernard Quancard:

First: get the procurement dashboard, look at it, remember it. Let me tell a brief story. As a SAM I once went to a large automotive company and was received by procurement. I said, "What the heck, why should I go there? They want to purchase a bunch of motor composites, pretty much commodity products; why should I bother?" Well, it turns out that the purchasing guy's spreadsheet has 12 lines. What are these lines? They're price, product lifecycle, maintenance cost, quality, delivery reliability, adaptability of the product, and six other items. Twelve lines! Price is only one of these. And you could match one internal stakeholder in the organization to each of these lines. The process engineer was most interested in quality and the cost of quality control, the logistics person most interested in delivery reliability, and so on. But in total there were 12 influencers on the purchase decision of this apparent commodity product, and the purchase decision was much more complex than just lowest price.

So, you have to begin to understand the dashboard of the customer procurement organization, which many people don't understand and don't even know. They presume it's only price.

Once you've done this, you have to say: "How can I create value in one element which is not price which will create significant quantifiable value for one of the key stakeholders in this decision?" You have to map key influencers: "Among the many potential ways to create value for stakeholders, where, specifically, is the biggest opportunity to create quantifiable business value?" You must focus on a limited number of stakeholders for whom you create a substantial amount of financial business value. You must map and work with key influencers, even if doing so means bypassing procurement.

Andreas Hinterhuber:

Excellent.

Bernard Quancard:

This means that in order to change the procurement dashboard you have to influence the part of the dashboard where you create the most value. Hopefully, the importance of this part of the dashboard will expand as you undergo the journey of strategic value creation with the customer.

So, it's a value journey. The end game of strategic account management is to manage the customer through a value journey rather than through a bunch of projects. It's a very different mindset. So I recommend influencing critical stakeholders for whom you create substantial quantified business value: these stakeholders will then change the procurement dashboard. The more value you create together, the more the customer's dashboard will change in your favor.

Andreas Hinterhuber:

Excellent. The starting point is an understanding of the customer's procurement dashboard. I'd add that in many consulting projects, my colleagues and I spend a substantial amount of time with procurement. First you understand; then you influence.

Bernard Quancard:

The problem is that many sales managers or SAMs do not know and do not even want to know the procurement dashboard. To them "it's all about price," but this is just an assumption.

Andreas Hinterhuber:

That's true. Do you have any further thoughts on the implementation of a commercial excellence or pricing strategy?

Bernard Quancard:

I'll begin with one barrier to the implementation of commercial excellence programs: the sales force. In many instances sales managers do not believe that value co-creation with customers is possible or profitable. This belief is not so easy to dismiss because there will always be some purely transactional, commodity-type business with some customers. But there will also always be customers who seek innovation, insights, expertise. Here we can and should co-create value. These customers want value, not price. So one obstacle to value co-creation is the mindset of sales and strategic account managers. Ultimately it comes down to senior executives, the CEO and the SVP of sales and marketing. Senior leaders have to be passionate that value co-creation is the way to grow part of the business. And this passionate belief is not always there: in this sense, the absence of a passionate belief is a barrier to value co-creation.

Another barrier is the attempt to co-create value with customers who don't want to co-create value: they only want to commoditize the supply chain. These customers to me are not strategic customers, so they should be treated in a purely transactional way and eventually through the internet. Selecting the right customers for value co-creation is a vitally important step before launching a commercial excellence or pricing program. Customers have to be open to strategic partnerships.

The third barrier is the talent. If, as you say, we re-brand sales managers as SAMs, we are bound to fail, because they lack the capabilities and talent needed to perform well as SAMs.

A final barrier are pricing capabilities: many companies do not provide the core SAM teams with the necessary pricing capabilities – coming from the other parts of the company – that are required to implement pricing strategies.

Andreas Hinterhuber:

In other words: senior managers need to ensure that SAMs have access to pricing capabilities by, for example, appointing a chief pricing officer. A head of pricing or chief pricing officer can collect and develop data, best practices, quantified value propositions, ROI case studies, discounting guidelines – all of which are very helpful in implementing pricing strategies. Senior managers create the organization and infrastructure, and SAMs can then access the required capabilities.

Bernard Quancard:

Absolutely.

Andreas Hinterhuber:

Bernard, thank you very much. I've really enjoyed this challenging and inspiring exchange on implementing pricing strategies. Thank you for this privilege.

Bernard Quancard:

Thank you, Andreas. I always appreciate our exchange of ideas.

Reference

Hinterhuber, A., and Kemps, P. (2017). "Interview: The ring of truth – value quantification in B2B services." In A. Hinterhuber and T. Snelgrove (Eds.), *Value First, then Price: Quantifying Value in Business Markets from the Perspective of Both Buyers and Sellers*, Milton Park, UK: Routledge, pp. 161–77.

6 Designing sales force compensation programs to improve pricing execution

Stephan M. Liozu

Introduction

Over the past 10 years, the pricing discipline has made great inroads (Hinterhuber and Liozu 2012b). More and more firms are adopting modern pricing practices (Liozu 2016), new pricing models are emerging to complement new-to-the-world business models (Hinterhuber and Liozu 2014), customer value quantification is becoming a hot topic (Johansson et al. 2015), and collaboration between pricing and sales teams has greatly increased (Hinterhuber and Liozu 2015).

Despite these major advancements, we have much work to do to embed pricing in the minds of top leaders as a top priority for growth and profitability. Even when they get started, companies find themselves stuck in a zone of good intentions (Hinterhuber and Liozu 2012a). Having great plans and pricing strategies is only half the battle. Executing them is another story (Liozu 2015b). Both price setting and price getting are necessary to deliver the impact that top leaders expect (Liozu and Hinterhuber 2014). One challenge is getting the sales force on board (Liozu 2015a) and implementing the right compensation plans to motivate the sales team to embrace and execute pricing tactics (Pollono 2015).

Sales compensation is often mentioned in practitioner circles as one of the major issues facing pricing and sales operations teams. The pricing and sales literature is silent on the topic of sales force compensation to drive pricing execution. Over the years, scholars have addressed issues of pricing authority (Homburg et al. 2005), pricing delegation (Frenzen et al. 2010; Lal 1986; Mishra and Prasad 2004), and pricing confidence (Liozu 2015c; Liozu and Hinterhuber 2013). For the most part, discussion of sales force compensation and pricing has been delegated to pricing consulting firms and practitioner circles.

To close this gap, semi-structured interviews were conducted with 12 executives in business-to-business (B2B) companies who have direct responsibility for and oversight of pricing and compensations plans. The interviews were conducted by telephone with the purpose of discovering best practices and critical considerations when designing sales force compensation plans to drive pricing execution.

The findings highlight the difficulties of changing sales force compensation in general. The experts agree that pricing cannot be the primary variable in what they call a basket of variables. Due to the considerable change-management challenge in changing sales force compensation, they recommend adding a pricing key performance indicator (KPI) as a third item in the basket. They also propose that having accurate data is key to driving pricing execution. Finally, driving pricing execution through changes in sales force compensation requires tremendous change-management support. Changes should be incremental and take place over a period of two to three years.

Prior research

The literature is rich in papers related to sales force compensation, performance-based programs, and individual performance drivers of sales representatives. The pricing literature generally discusses pricing centralization, delegation of pricing authority, and price realization without offering any broad perspective on the impact of sales force compensation plans. Literature focusing on both sales force compensation and pricing is scarce. Most scholars have focused on peripheral and important dimensions impacting compensation systems. For example, strategic misalignment can lead to pricing issues and potential irrational pricing decisions (Liozu 2013a, b). Misalignment of organizational incentives and goal systems is often mentioned as contributing to organizational tensions and potential challenges to performance (Kerr 1975; Hinterhuber 2008). "Rewarding A while hoping for B" (Kerr 1975: 1) potentially leads to misaligned incentive systems and to the creation of organizational frictions in the firm (Barnard and Andrews 1968: 139). Incentive systems designed by top management can serve either to "sharpen or to blunt their decisive effectiveness" (Walton and Dutton 1969: 75) depending on the background of the top leaders and their track record should they come from a sales background (Pollono 2015).

The literature on pricing, and specifically on the deployment and assimilation of value-based pricing programs, suggests that reward systems based on pricing and profit need to be formalized and implemented across the organization to break down silo thinking and remediate a potential lack of accountability (Hinterhuber 2004, 2008). Getting the sales force to buy in to a new compensation program focused on profitability requires involving more than just the sales force (Liozu 2015b). A value-based transformation requires value-based incentives across the organization to generate an army of value merchants (Anderson et al. 2007). These value-based incentives must be based on performance-oriented goals – most likely as revenue, margin, growth, pricing – to drive positive change in sales force behaviors and focus (Kohli et al. 1998; Coughlan and Joseph 2012; Silver et al. 2006). Other research findings also indicate that sales incentives are critical to successful pricing transformation (Liozu et al. 2011). It is essential that sales and account management be rewarded based on appropriate performance criteria and also have "skin in the game" (Liozu and Hinterhuber 2013).

Finally, pricing consulting firms have designed highly technical methodologies for creating data-driven sales force compensation plans to improve price realization (Soulliard 2010; Zuponcic 2013). These methodologies offer customized approaches to firms interested in changing their sales force compensation plans. Although these are useful, consultants do not propose generalizable and research-based approaches to deploying new compensation systems that include a pricing component.

About the research

Qualitative interviews were conducted with 12 pricing and marketing executives from large B2B organizations (see Table 6.1). The intention was to select senior executives with experience in designing, influencing, and deploying sales force compensation programs.

Participants were selected based on their organizational seniority and their organization's pricing maturity. Selections were validated by the president of the Professional Pricing Society.

The primary method of data collection was semi-structured interviews conducted over a 3-month period, from April to June 2014. Twelve interviews were conducted by telephone at the respondents' place of employment. The interviews, averaging 30-plus

Table 6.1 Sample of respondents

Respondent	Title	Industry	Size
1	VP of Pricing	Medical equipment	>10,000 employees
2	Director of Pricing	Telecom equipment	>10,000 employees
3	Director of Pricing	Safety equipment	5,000 to 10,000 employees
4	Director of Corporate Pricing	Chemicals	>10,000 employees
5	Director of Marketing	Medical equipment	>10,000 employees
6	VP of Pricing and Customer Excellence	Tool and equipment	>10,000 employees
7	VP of Corporate Pricing	Heavy industrial products	>10,000 employees
8	VP of Pricing	Specialty medical products	>10,000 employees
9	VP of Pricing	Chemicals	>10,000 employees
10	VP of Pricing & Customer Analytics	Knowledge intelligence services	>10,000 employees
11	Operating Partner – Pricing & Analytics	Private equity firm	5,000 to 10,000 employees
12	Director of Value Realization	Building materials	Under 1,000 employees

minutes, were digitally recorded and subsequently transcribed by a professional service organization. The focus was on these executives' experiences in addressing pricing execution and with designing modern and progressive sales force compensation plans to help execution. Interviewers asked open-ended questions to motivate rich and specific narratives, and used probes when necessary to clarify and amplify responses.

Consistent with thematic data analysis techniques (Boyatzis 1998), transcripts were reviewed and treated through several rounds of coding to identify relevant themes.

Findings

The findings unveil the complexity of changing sales force compensation plans in general. There is added complexity in tying sales force performance to pricing performance, which requires intense preparation and supposes control over data, systems, and financial models. Finally, as with any transformational program, changing sales force compensation to improve pricing execution requires a great deal of change management.

Finding 1: Any change in sales force compensation plans is emotional, sensitive, and potentially explosive; it must be handled with extreme care

All respondents agree that changing sales force compensation plans is a sensitive and potentially explosive effort. There is nothing easy about messing around with the earning potential of a sales team:

> It's enormously sensitive. I was on commission for 12 years as a salesperson. My sales compensation was changed twice. Both times, I made more money from the change. Both times, I was furious and thought my bosses were trying to cheat me. And I don't think I am a crazy emotional person, but it's incredibly sensitive.
>
> (Respondent 1)

> You are messing around with someone's pay. So that really gets people nervous when you start messing around it.
>
> (Respondent 3)

> I think some of this is just trying to keep the peace. It is trying to maintain harmony with the sales force because anytime you start monkeying around with someone's compensation, that is pretty sensitive.
>
> (Respondent 4)

Adding a pricing component to a sales force compensation program can add complexity, as pricing is often considered a complex process:

> Changing the sales force compensation is not an easy proposition, especially when you want to include pricing components to variable pay. Both are explosive topics, and you have to prepare well.
>
> (Respondent 12)

Considering the emotional nature of the topic, most respondents agree that there is much more to designing sales force compensation plans with a pricing component than the mere technical aspects. The human and emotional aspects of the change need to be factored in, too.

Finding 2: Improving pricing execution with the sales force requires a change in the target variables; developing a basket of variables seems a good approach; and including a pricing KPI in this basket improves pricing execution

On the technical front of the discussion, 11 of 12 respondents agree that a sales force compensation plan that includes a pricing component has to be set up as a basket of variables, as shown in Table 6.2. The ideal number of variables is two or three.

Table 6.2 Structure of compensation plan for greater pricing execution

Respondent	Number of variables in basket	Variables	Weight distribution	Capping?	Escalator/de-escalator?
1	3	Volume/growth/price	50%/40%/10%	No	Yes
2	3	Total sales revenues/margin/price	50%/25%/25%	N/A	N/A
3	3	Total revenues/margin/pricing	50%/35%/15%	No	Yes
4	1	Contribution margin	50% individual/50% BU*	No	Yes
5	3	Margin/total revenue/price	50%/40%/10%	Yes	Yes
6	3	Total revenue/average discount/price	60%/20%/20%	No	Yes
7	2	Volume/sales mix/price	50%/25%/25%	No	Yes
8	3	Revenue/new client acquisition/price	60%/20%/20%	No	Yes
9	2	Sales revenue/EBITDA**	50%/50%	N/A	N/A
10	3	Revenue/growth/price	50%/30%/20%	No	Yes
11	3	Volume/gross margin/price	75%/15%/10%	No	Yes
12	3	Total revenue/margin/price	50%/30%/20%	No	Yes

* BU: Business unit.
** EBITDA: Earnings before interests, taxes, depreciations, and amortizations.

Because sales reps are sales reps, most respondents agree that volume, or total sales revenues, should remain the largest component of variable compensation. Ten of twelve respondents declare that volume and total sales revenues need to remain the primary target and assigned the highest weight in the basket (50–75 percent). Most of the respondents also agree that there should be no capping of compensation plans when they are allowed to drive improved pricing execution. Similarly, most respondents are in favor of using escalator and de-escalator mechanisms to promote pricing and margin performance.

When asked what might be the most appropriate pricing KPI to use in a variable basket, most respondents consider year-on-year improvements in pricing to be relevant (see Table 6.3).

This pricing variable would be introduced as a third component of a basket and would represent 10 to 25 percent of the overall variable potential, as shown in Table 6.2.

Finding 3: Changing sales force compensation to drive pricing execution cannot be done overnight; time to transition is necessary

Changing sales force compensation to drive pricing execution cannot happen overnight. Ten of twelve respondents agree that a transition time of two to three years is needed (see Table 6.4). Two respondents prefer a "big bang" approach to make the change once and for all.

Table 6.3 Recommended pricing KPI

Respondent	Pricing KPIs
1	List price realization
2	"Price quality": actual average sales versus plan
3	Year-on-year average discount improvement
4	Value realization (using EVE®)
5	Price realization versus prior year
6	Average sales price (ASP)
7	Year-on-year change in pricing
8	"Price erosion": year-on-year ASP
9	EBITDA
10	Year-on-year ASP
11	ASP – deal pricing realization versus expected
12	Year-on-year ASP and discount improvement

Table 6.4 Recommended transition time

Respondent	Transition time
1	2 to 3 years
2	3 years
3	At least 2 years
4	2 to 3 years
5	2 years
6	Big bang – 3 years of preparation
7	Big bang
8	3 years
9	2 to 3 years
10	2 to 3 years
11	2 to 3 years
12	3 years

A transition time is necessary to deploy the changes incrementally and to show that the new compensation plan is neutral:

> We run dual compensation for 6 to 12 months and we pay them the most. So we run it both ways for that period of time. We are going to show that it is pretty neutral, but for 6 to 12 months we will pay you whatever is more or we will pay you the old way.
> (Respondent 3)

> It is like the old Change Management 101 that just says 'be incremental so that you can phase the changes in'.
> (Respondent 11)

> We have changed compensation over three years to let the sales organization adjust to it and to also prevent any major disruption in the business.
> (Respondent 12)

Finding 4: Improving pricing execution using sales force compensation requires change management at all levels; things do not happen overnight, and good preparation is key

All respondents declare that change management should be taken seriously when adapting sales force compensation plans to strategic profit priorities. Table 6.5 shows an overview of answers by respondents and by priority when they were asked what critical change-management considerations are important to the deployment of new plans.

Roles of top sales leaders. Consistent with previous research on top management championing of pricing efforts, our respondents often mention the role of top sales leadership

Table 6.5 Change-management considerations

Respondent	First	Second	Third
1	Pilot studies	Financial models	Psychology of winning
2	Top sales leadership on board	Lots of examples	Confidence in data
3	Strategic contextualization	Reassurance on fair transition	Top sales leadership on board
4	Strong case for change	Data accuracy	Fair process with exceptions
5	Strategic contextualization	Data accuracy and transparency	Simplicity of the program
6	Confidence in data	CEO and C-suite support	Fair process with bridging
7	Top sales leadership on board	Clear direction in the process	Simplicity in KPIs
8	Accuracy of data and systems	Design plan with sales force	Top sales leadership on board
9	Strategic contextualization	Aligned goals and objectives	Long-term orientation
10	Simplicity of the program	Strategic contextualization	Design committee with sales
11	Align business and compensation strategies	Financial models to test	Early stakeholder on boarding
12	Top sales leadership on board	Change communication	Tools, models, and data in place

(5 of 12) in the successful deployment of sales force compensation plans for superior pricing execution:

> Change management is a huge undergoing. You have to have complete buy-in. Sales leadership has to believe in what you are doing, and you have to be able to link it directly back to the overall strategic vision of the business and what the financial impact objectives are for the business.
>
> (Respondent 2)

> Without the top-level sales – not just the CEO saying it is a good idea and the president who supports it – it is not going to fly. You are going to be struggling.
>
> (Respondent 3)

> What top sales leaders are saying is that the pain is not greater than the gain. They say, 'We have looked at this, and the pain of change is too big for the gain we expect to get.'
>
> (Respondent 5)

Strategic contextualization. Similarly, 4 of 12 respondents mention the need to contextualize the changes in sales force compensation for greater pricing execution in the overall strategic story of the firm:

> We did it just as compensation, but that probably is the wrong way to do it. It should have been explained as part of the bigger strategy.
>
> (Respondent 3)

> I think, first off, in an ideal world, it is an end-to-end process where you start with the right strategy with the right policies and with the right compensation plans. And your compensation should move your strategic objectives.
>
> (Respondent 5)

> The business strategy is what is going to set your [compensation] objectives. We would then bring the tools and capabilities to measure and communicate how effective they are doing that.
>
> (Respondent 9)

Need for simplicity. Keeping the new compensation plan simple was mentioned by 3 of 12 respondents:

> So I think you have to have your special sessions with lots of examples. And again, make it as simple as possible so that it can be implemented.
>
> (Respondent 2)

> So we tweaked compensation. It was too complicated ... My recommendation is to choose one system that is simple enough.
>
> (Respondent 5)

> Sales teams are very fickle. You want to give them notice but not too much. You want the CEO saying the same thing as the head of sales. You want the message to be simple. Some of it, you need to dumb it down. Two dimensions are better than eighteen.
>
> (Respondent 11)

Finally, one respondent highlighted the need to play on the competitiveness of the sales force as a way to drive great sales at a higher price:

> Any time I am working with the salespeople, I am always talking about winning. I always use the word 'winning' because that is what they want to do. Any salesperson would prefer to win at a higher price and brag about that.
>
> (Respondent 1)

Finding 5: Without proper data, you will not be able to gain the confidence of your sales force; pricing is often considered a black box; data and systems are the backbone of your change process

In line with the latest finding, where 6 respondents of 12 mention the need for accurate data (see Table 6.5), respondents listed some of the questions they had to ask themselves in preparation for their sales force compensation transition plans, as shown in Table 6.6.

In general, all respondents agree that much attention should be paid to the accuracy of the data, as highlighted next:

> You are cobbling something together that is not originally designed to [be cobbled together]. You are not certain of the absolute accuracy of that. And you are paying people based on stuff that might not be perfectly accurate.
>
> (Respondent 1)

> You have to make sure that you can do it correctly, because salespeople are very quick. They look at the data that is being used to justify the payout and challenge it.
>
> (Respondent 4)

Table 6.6 List of critical questions about data

1	Do I have reasonably *clean* transactional data?
2	Do I have clean *structured* pricing data?
3	Can I *replicate* the sales force informal compensation calculations?
4	Can I replicate and project current compensation levels using existing data?
5	Do I have the proper *systematic* tools and methods in place across all sales groups?
6	Do I sufficiently understand the *subjective* mechanisms that impact sales force compensations?
7	Do I fully understand customer *mix*, product mix, true pricing effect?
8	Do I have the right data to *model* future KPIs and drive behavior?
9	Is the data *readily available* to be able to dynamically inform the sales force on performance under new plan?
10	Have I sufficiently taken into account qualitative information (exceptions, deviations, special contracts)?

You start getting into 'is the data available?' And things start falling off the rails right here. So you conclude that it is too much of a headache, too much risk, and that we do not have the data. Because if you do not have the data, you will always have sales reps arguing with you.

(Respondent 6)

All respondents mentioned the dimension of data accuracy and transparency necessary to give the sales force confidence that the addition of pricing to the basket of variables is not only accurate but also fair. That notion of fairness is reflected in some of the answers listed in Table 6.5.

Conclusions and discussion

This research project highlights some of the key considerations in changing sales force compensation plans to drive greater pricing execution. Based on the state of prior research and insights from 12 top executives, the following conclusions are drawn.

First, a highlight is the fact that a basket of variables is the most appropriate way to add a pricing KPI to the variable-compensation equation. Moving from a single variable to a multi-variable basket requires proper attention to detail, as shown in the list of key questions to think about proposed in Figure 6.1.

Essential to the discussion is selecting the proper pricing KPI and defining the proper distribution of weights in the basket. The selection of the variables to be included in the plan also might lead to the question of data availability and accuracy, as suggested by our respondents. This conclusion supports previous findings from other pricing scholars who have highlighted the strong need for alignment between business priorities and sales force compensation (Liozu 2015a; Pollono 2015). It also suggests that change management requires proper incentives to focus relevant stakeholders to the right reward system (Kerr 1975).

Second, it is proposed that redesigning a sales force compensation plan to include a pricing component requires a transition and a change-management process. Based on the respondents' insights, the following three steps are proposed, as shown in Figure 6.2.

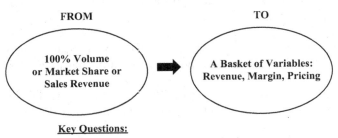

Key Questions:
1) How many variables in the basket?
2) What distribution between variables?
3) When to change? At once or incrementally?
4) Do I have the data ready to do changes?
5) How do I bridge change years?

Figure 6.1 A compensation based on a basket of variables.

Step 1: Preparation
1) Understand current process across all sales groups.
2) Evaluate the level of data readiness for change.
3) Clean the data before doing anything else.
4) Engage sales leadership and HR on the design of the plan.
5) Communicate the burning platform for the need for comp change.

Step 2: Design and Testing
1) Crystallize new sales compensation plan (SCP).
2) Finalize change roadmap with required change tools.
3) Build systematic tool/model for existing and new comp plans.
4) Model new SCP with existing sales data for all sales reps.
5) Model new SCP with n+1 budgeted sales for all sales reps.

Step 3: Start Deployment
1) Tie phase 1 of deployment to new budget cycle.
2) Train, train, train, train and train more early in the process.
3) Use models to reassure sales force with rational data.
4) Proactively tackle the special issues and circumstances.
5) Explain tools, models, mechanics, data readiness, etc.

Figure 6.2 Incremental change process.

Step 1 focuses on understanding the current situation and forming a burning platform for change, which might include the strategic contextualization often mentioned by the respondents. Step 1 also identifies and prepares relevant data. Step 2 focuses on designing and testing the new sales force compensation plan by developing the change roadmap and designing the relevant financial models to project the future for the sales force. Step 3 focuses on deploying and engaging the sales force to build their confidence and help them assimilate the new plans. This transitional model focuses on all the critical considerations proposed by the respondents in Table 6.5. It also allows pricing and sales leadership to build the right level of confidence in the sales team (Liozu 2015c) so that they do not feel cheated in any way. A transitional model creates a sense of rationality as they see the small changes in incentives plans without negative effect (Liozu 2015b).

Third, it is proposed that the factors critical to successfully designing a pricing execution-focus plan relate mostly to preparation and change management, as shown in Figure 6.3.

One might argue that this list could be applied to any redesign of sales force compensation plans and not just to those that might include a pricing component. I agree. But considering the emotional nature of pricing in general and the lack of pricing data in organizations, it is necessary to reinforce the need for extra preparation and change management preparation. Bringing the sales force on board during the design phase of the new plan is essential (Liozu 2015a).

> 1. Data, data, data and **data**!
> 2. Understand where you are **starting** from.
> 3. Prepare a **roadmap** for compensation adaptation.
> 4. Create **advanced models** to project variations, to duplicate current and future plans and to identify outliers.
> 5. Get **all levels of sales** involved in the change design.
> 6. **Communicate** extensively across the board.
> 7. Use all of your change-management **toolbox**.
> 8. Do not **rush** the process or be too process-oriented.
> 9. Be transparent, clear, mindful, **fair** and consistent.
> 10. Remember that the last thing you need is a sales force **revolt**.

Figure 6.3 Key success factors for sales compensation plans.

Fourth, and finally, this research also highlights the need for further discussion on the role of sales force compensation to drive pricing execution. The words of Respondent 7 summarize this well:

> I think people want a magic measure to help them make perfect decisions and it does not exist. There is too much noise. There are too many bad behaviors. When somebody says 'I just want a better compensation system', what they are really saying is 'I do not want to manage prices'. All of that together and 'we still want to manage price through sales for incentives'. To me that does not make sense. To me I would rather say 'pay them any way you want, just do not let them make a price decision'.

In other words, do we manage the issue of price delegation or the issue of sales force compensation to drive pricing performance? Is the gain greater than the gain? Should we make all pricing decisions for the sales force and let them execute with no deviations? These questions calls for further research on the trade-off between price delegation (Bhardwaj 2001) and sales force compensation (Pollono 2015).

Limitations and future research

These findings should be reviewed in light of several limitations. The sample included only large B2B firms hand-selected based on their pricing maturity and the seniority of their executives. Including other sectors and firm sizes might yield different findings. The researchers have significant experience in and knowledge of B2B pricing, especially in the area of pricing strategies and tactics. However, to remain mindful of the risk of bias (Corbin and Strauss 2008), open-ended questions were used to elicit rich, unstructured responses to capture respondents' experiences and stories (Maxwell 2005), interpretations and understandings of pricing challenges and sales force resistance.

The intention with this qualitative study was to establish a platform for future research. The impact of sales force compensation plans on pricing execution should be studied more consistently across regions and sectors. There is a need to demonstrate a direct relationship between price-driven sales force compensation plans and firm performance (Coughlan and Joseph 2012). The role of top sales leadership in driving changes to sales force compensation plans also deserves some attention. It is hoped that this study stimulates the desire of scholars to further investigate the topic.

References

Anderson, J. C., Kumar, N. and Narus, J. A. (2007) *Value Merchants: Demonstrating and Documenting Superior Value in Business Markets*, Boston, MA: Harvard Business School Press.

Barnard, C. and Andrews, K. (1968) *The Functions of the Executive*, Boston, MA: Harvard University Press.

Bhardwaj, P. (2001) "Delegating pricing decisions," *Marketing Science* 20(2): 143–69.

Boyatzis, R. (1998) *Transforming Qualitative Information: Thematic Analysis and Code Development*, Thousand Oaks, CA: Sage Publications.

Corbin, J. and Strauss, A. (2008) *Basics of Qualitative Research*, Newbury Park, CA: Sage Publications.

Coughlan, A. T. and Joseph, K. (2012) "Sales force compensation: Research insights and research potential," in: Lillien, G. and Grewal, R. (eds.) *Handbook on Business-to-Business Marketing*, Northampton, MA: Edward Elgar, pp. 473–495.

Frenzen, H., Hansen, A., Krafft, M., Mantrala, M. and Schmidt, S. (2010) "Delegation of pricing authority to the sales force: An agency-theoretic perspective of its determinants and impact on performance", *International Journal of Research in Marketing* 27(1): 58–68.

Hinterhuber, A. (2004) "Towards value-based pricing – An integrative framework for decision making," *Industrial Marketing Management* 33(8): 765–78.

Hinterhuber, A. (2008) "Customer value-based pricing strategies: Why companies resist," *Journal of Business Strategy* 29(4): 41–50.

Hinterhuber, A. and Liozu, S. M. (2012a) "Is it time to rethink your pricing strategy?" *MIT Sloan Management Review* 53(4): 69–77.

Hinterhuber, A. and Liozu, S. M. (2012b) *Innovation in Pricing: Contemporary Theories and Best Practices*, Abingdon, UK: Routledge.

Hinterhuber, A. and Liozu, S. M. (2014) 'Is innovation in pricing your next source of competitive advantage?', *Business Horizons* 57(3): 413–23.

Hinterhuber, A. and Liozu, S. M. (2015) *Pricing and the Sales Force*, Abingdon, UK: Routledge.

Homburg, C., Hoyer, W. D. and Koschate, N. (2005) "Customers' reactions to price increases: Do customer satisfaction and perceived motive fairness matter?" *Journal of the Academy of Marketing Science* 33(1): 36–49.

Johansson, M., Keränen, J., Hinterhuber, A., Liozu, S. and Andersson, L. (2015) 'Value assessment and pricing capabilities – How to profit from value," *Journal of Revenue & Pricing Management* 14(3): 178–97.

Kerr, S. (1975) "On the folly of rewarding A, while hoping for B," *The Academy of Management Journal* 18(4): 769–83.

Kohli, A. K., Shervani, T. A. and Challagalla, G. N. (1998) "Learning and performance orientation of salespeople: The role of supervisors," *Journal of Marketing Research* 35(2): 263–74.

Lal, R. (1986) "Technical note – Delegating pricing responsibility to the salesforce," *Marketing Science* 5(2): 159–68.

Liozu, S., Boland, R. J. J., Hinterhuber, A. and Perelli, S. (2011) "Industrial pricing orientation: The organizational transformation to value-based pricing," International Conference on Engaged Management Scholarship, June, Case Western Reserve University, Cleveland, OH, pp. 41–48.

Liozu, S. M. (2013a) "Do you have a pricing problem?" *Pricing Advisor* (March): 5–6.

Liozu, S. M. (2013b) "Irrational pricing decisions in organizations," *Journal of Professional Pricing* Q2: 13–19.

Liozu, S. M. (2015a) "Getting the sales force on board," in: Hinterhuber, A. and Liozu, S. M. (eds.) *Pricing and the Sales Force*, Abingdon, UK: Routledge.

Liozu, S. M. (2015b) *"The Pricing Journey: The Organizational Transformation Toward Pricing Excellence,"* Stanford, CA: Stanford University Press.

Liozu, S. M. (2015c) "Pricing superheroes: How a confident sales team can influence firm performance," *Industrial Marketing Management* 47: 26–38.

Liozu, S. M. (2016) 'The evolution and future of pricing capabilities," *Journal of Revenue and Pricing Management* 15(3): 306–16.

Liozu, S. M. and Hinterhuber, A. (2013) "The confidence factor in pricing: Driving firm performance," *Journal of Business Strategy* 34(4): 11–21.

Liozu, S. M. and Hinterhuber, A. (2014) *The ROI of Pricing: Measuring the Impact and Making the Business Case*, Abingdon, UK: Routledge.

Maxwell, J. (2005) *Qualitative Research Design: An Interactive Approach* (Vol. 42), Thousand Oaks, CA: Sage Publications.

Mishra, B. K. and Prasad, A. (2004) "Centralized pricing versus delegating pricing to the salesforce under information asymmetry," *Marketing Science* 23(1): 21–27.

Pollono, E. (2015) "Pricing delegation and sales force compensation," in: Hinterhuber, A. and Liozu, S. M. (eds.) *Pricing and the Sales Force*, Abingdon, UK: Routledge, pp. 161–171.

Silver, L. S., Dwyer, S. and Alford, B. (2006) "Learning and performance goal orientation of salespeople revisited: The role of performance-approach and performance-avoidance orientations," *Journal of Personal Selling and Sales Management* 26(1): 27–38.

Soulliard, A. (2010) The last mile for pricing performance: Compensating your sales force for price realization. Professional Pricing Society Annual Conference, Brussels, Belgium.

Walton, R. and Dutton, J. (1969) "The management of interdepartmental conflict: A model and review," *Administrative Science Quarterly* 14(1): 73–84.

Zuponcic, R. 2013. "How to reward your sales team for price performance," available from: http://pricepointpartners.com/blog/reward-sales-team-for-price-performance.

Part 4
Pricing strategy implementation
The role of marketing

Part 4

7 Implementing pricing strategy by developing and implementing effective discounting practices

Evandro Pollono and Jose Vela

> This interview discusses the critical role of sales managers in pricing strategy implementation. Analytical skills and the ability to analyze and make sense of big data are increasingly important. Sales managers should not merely execute, but lead the overall transformation related to a change in pricing strategy.

Evandro Pollono:

Describe your role in the process of pricing strategy implementation.

Jose Vela:

Let me also briefly introduce myself. I studied mathematics at the University of Barcelona. I've been in management positions, mainly as general manager, for more than 15 years. I ran a very successful pricing improvement project three years ago in the country I was managing, and one year ago the CEO of my company offered me the job of director of pricing of the group. The Spandex Group is a B2B [business-to-business] company present in Europe and Australia. We have offices and warehouses in 15 countries, and we are one of the world's leading suppliers of materials, sign systems, displays, and equipment to the sign-making and graphics industries.

Working very closely with the CEO and the CFO of Spandex, I am responsible for defining and implementing the common pricing strategy for the whole group.

Because we operate in very different countries with very different go-to-market approaches, we see ourselves as a "federation of companies" and not as a "monolithic" group; therefore, the "last mile" of the strategy implementation is the responsibility of each country manager.

To implement our pricing strategy, we determine at the group level which processes, tools, and reports we will use, and we provide the vision, guidance, and training that our country managers and sales managers need to maximize our revenue and profits through pricing improvement actions.

I also see myself as a sort of "pricing evangelist" in the group. I love sharing best practices and success stories about how pricing power can boost profits, margins, and earnings before interest, tax, depreciation, and amortization (EBITDA).

Evandro Pollono:

Let's begin by discussing the *general* capabilities of sales managers (those that define what it takes to perform well in sales). What do you see as major changes between current/past capabilities and the capabilities that are required in the future?

Jose Vela:

Current capabilities are just "old" ones (such as people management, interpersonal skills, forecasting, follow-up and tracking, …) plus the following:

Change management: it's always been a vital skill, but now, considering the speed of changes and the generational challenges (baby boomers vs. millennials, digital natives vs. non-digital natives, …) mastering this capability is key.

Analytical skills: the ability to extract information from data and, on top of this, to make it actionable is vital in today's business world full of spreadsheets and business intelligence reports.

Being process-oriented, very responsive to market changes, and curious about new ways to improve and maximize the business is also mandatory in current professional environments.

Evandro Pollono:

What's your take on pricing authority for sales managers? Under which circumstances do you favor a broad/narrow pricing authority? What level of discounting authority works best?

Jose Vela:

As I explained, we see ourselves as a "federation of companies." Therefore, we delegate much pricing authority to our country and sales managers.

Nobody will never ever catch me – or anyone on my team – asking for approval in a local pricing decision. Nevertheless, discount guidance tools and approval levels (Subfloor, Floor, Level 1, …) are at the group level.

We calculate these approval levels by segmenting all transactions by customer and product group sales. Figure 7.1 is an example of how we segment based on customer sales. As you can see, we compute for each country the sales contribution per customer and identify those customers that bring us 30 percent of our sales, 60 percent of our sales, and so forth. We end this process with five different customer-sales-based segments: very large, large, medium, small, and very small. We do the same at the product group level to create three more segments: A, B, and C. Therefore, for each product we have 15 segments in total (i.e., Very Large and A = VLA, Medium and C = MC, etc.) that bring us enough granularity to create meaningful discount corridors and approval levels, as shown in Figure 7.2.

From my own experience, I don't think there exists a "specific level of discounting authority" that works best. It's well established that you must analyze this case by case and, depending on the maturity of each organization, set the authorization thresholds accordingly.

Once you've decided on your delegation-of-authority model, you must run reports regularly to ensure that the sales team's compliance is good enough. I've seen in a few

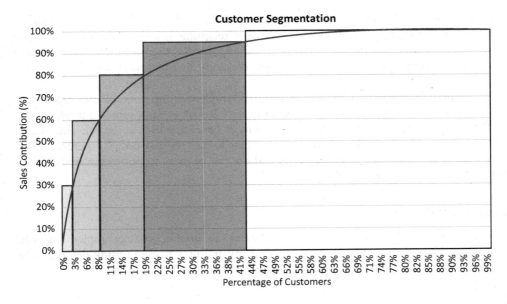

Figure 7.1 Customer Pareto analysis.

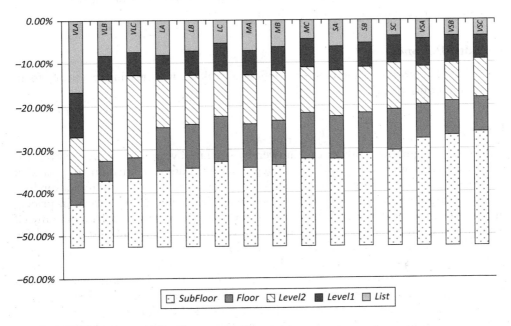

Figure 7.2 Discounting guidelines by customer segment.

companies that a discount guidance, a very well-established and successful pricing tactic, fails because salespeople were not following the recommendations. Discount corridors were well calculated, but people in the field had long trusted their instincts, and there was no clear indication from the top management to adopt discount corridors – so here you have a perfect storm.

To avoid such situations, I strongly recommend implementing a compliance report that shows how many discounts each sales representative has set at each approval level.

We've set a target of 70 percent of discounts at Level 2, which is the self-authorized level for our sales team. Does it make sense that a sales rep has only 27 percent of all given discounts at the self-approved level and the rest of them must be escalated? I don't think so.

Evandro Pollono:

Do you have examples of best-in-class companies in pricing strategy implementation? Or any learnings from outside your own company/industry that you think deserve to be considered when implementing pricing strategies?

Jose Vela:

I try to keep my eyes open, and I attend as many pricing conferences and webinars as I can, but more than a "best in class" approach, I tend to identify best practices and success stories that I try to tailor to our organization.

Evandro Pollono:

How should companies begin the journey from a weak focus on pricing to a strong focus to driving profits via pricing?

Jose Vela:

This is an easy question with an easy answer: by starting! I've seen so many medium-to-small companies without any pricing strategy that attribute this situation to a "lack of resources" or to the "high investment required" to buy a pricing solution from a vendor.

At the beginning of this interview, I mentioned that I ran a very successful pricing improvement project. I implemented in my company a peer pricing tool that I built myself while running the business as general manager. Moreover, I did it with just an Excel file and a basic knowledge of mathematical distributions.

Figure 7.3 is a screenshot of the distribution of a real product.

As you can see, you cover almost 80 percent of all the transactions with up to a 40 percent discount. Does it make sense to allow your sales representatives to give a higher discount without a solid story that supports that petition? I don't think so.

I guarantee you that with this basic transactional analysis and a simple customer segmentation based on percentiles, you can create a simplistic but fully functional discount guidance for your sales team. You'll have neither AI [artificial intelligence] nor ML [machine learning] – you won't even have elasticity – but it will do the job.

On top of this, adding end dates to all discounts will ensure that your sales team reviews the discounts and has meaningful business discussions with their customers.

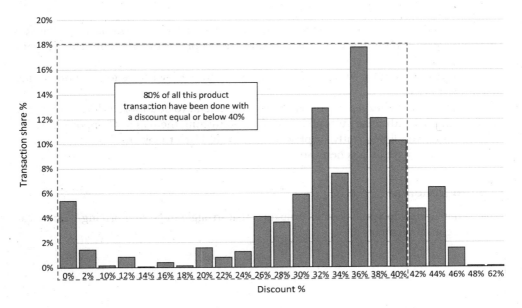

Figure 7.3 Pocket-price-band analysis.

Last but not least, ensure that your sales team is well equipped with solid price negotiation skills and, voilà, your pricing journey has just begun!

Evandro Pollono:

Let's get down to the individual sales managers. What in your view are the characteristics – personality traits – of sales managers who excel in pricing strategy implementation? What are, by contrast, the personality traits or behavioral characteristics that make the individual sales manager less effective?

Jose Vela:

They must be highly analytical but also able to understand the power and the benefits of using a sales strategy based on value instead of discounting, and able to coach and train their team in this direction.

By contrast, "old-school" sales managers who base their success and that of their sales team on selling "by relationship," who place more trust in perceptions than in facts, and who are unwilling to improve and learn are, by far, the least effective sales managers I've met.

Evandro Pollono:

Selling also means, to a degree, changing the decision criteria for the purchasing organization – which in some cases may be focused on price, price, and price alone. Can you share some insights on how to change the purchasing criteria of hard-nosed B2B purchasers?

Jose Vela:

I honestly don't think you can change anyone's purchasing decision criteria. But what you definitely *can* do is reinforce your strengths and raise your customer's confidence in your proposal.

For sure, there are what we call "opportunistic customers" who are focused on getting the cheapest price.

For us, being the cheapest is not an option, as we tend to add more value, so our only winning strategy with these customers is to (a) stop treating them as just "opportunistic" – and sometimes you'll be greatly surprised – and to (b) learn to say "no."

There are no silver bullets here. Sorry.

Evandro Pollono:

What other advice do you have for companies that struggle in getting pricing/value creation strategies implemented?

Jose Vela:

Begin.

Define a reduced scope for your first pricing project and enroll some pricing-enthusiastic business managers – there are some in every organization; you just need to look for them – and just begin.

Pricing projects tend to succeed – especially if you begin from the ground level – and it's easy to collect low-hanging fruit at first; with this success story in your backpack, you'll find it easier to recruit more people in your organization for your pricing crusade.

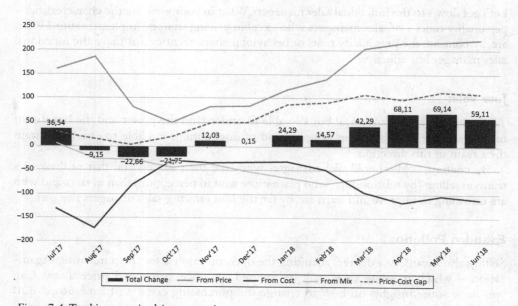

Figure 7.4 Tracking margin drivers over time.

You'll also need some reports to isolate the impact of pricing and to help managers visualize it. If you don't have it and just measure GM% [gross margin percent] improvement, credit for your pricing action may go to purchasing (lower costs) or to marketing (changes in product mix).

Figure 7.4 illustrates a GM% driver analysis. It's also a nice success story in one of our countries: they were struggling in terms of profits, so we helped the country and sales manager implement specific pricing actions that, in just 6 months, reversed the negative trend and helped them deliver a nice earnings before interest, taxes, depreciation and amortization (EBITDA) improvement.

Finally yet importantly, always credit the sales team for any pricing success because they are in charge of the "last mile" implementation, and their part is not the easiest.

Evandro Pollono:

Jose, I appreciate the privilege of sharing your expertise on pricing strategy implementation. Thank you.

8 Designing and executing B2B customer segmentation

Stephan M. Liozu and Katie Richardson

Introduction

Customer segmentation is at the heart of marketing. It's one of the most essential steps in progressive market management, and it's also one of the most neglected. By neglected, we mean that it's not performed at all, it's designed in a very traditional fashion using demographic or firmographic parameters, or it's designed but never operationalized. Over the last decade, the science and art of segmentation has evolved. Best-in-class organizations have embraced the scientific data revolution and have begun to design both qualitative and quantitative segmentation processes that leverage their rich data.

In both business-to-consumer (B2C) and business-to-business (B2B) markets, best-in-class organizations have quickly realized that the one-size-fits-all approach is no longer relevant. Progress in the science of segmentation and the availability of data allows marketers to better refine their segmentation depth. For example, there has been much media attention surrounding Netflix's lack of segmentation with its one-size-fits-all streaming offers and its pricing-level offers. Netflix is now trying to better segment its rich customer base to design a variety of content packages and bundles in various price ranges.

We could write a whole book on segmentation types and techniques. In fact, there are already a number of books published on this subject. But that's not why we're writing this chapter. We've conducted dozens of quantitative and qualitative customer-segmentation projects, and the segmentation science is difficult to grasp. Each project is different and encounters unique challenges. In the spirit of sharing some of the best practices, we focus on four considerations that are essential to successful customer segmentation: leveraging customer data, conducting segmentation with qualitative information, positioning segmentation as a cost-optimization program to improve adoption, and operationalizing segmentation in a business. Let's begin!

A refresher on B2B customer segmentation

Not all segmentations are created equal

Customer segmentation is not product, price, or strategic segmentation. These are different techniques requiring different analyses by different stakeholders. Most of the time, all segmentation should be done in parallel during the strategic-planning process, the marketing-planning process, or as part of pricing strategy. But customer segmentation is about taking a full population of customers or a subset of that population (existing vs. lost vs. prospects) and classifying them into homogeneous groups based on their product usage, buying behaviors, preferences, and needs. This is different from product segmentation or market segmentation. Definitions matter when working in advanced marketing. Still, many companies don't conduct in-depth and dynamic customer segmentation as part of their marketing-planning process. That leads to potential issues, as listed in Figure 8.1.

The data matters

Big data in marketing and sales allows for micro-segmentation and more relevant one-on-one marketing. You might not realize it, but you already have all the data required to conduct a basic segmentation analysis: survey data, quality data, transactional data, website traffic data, and so forth. The data might be fragmented rather than centralized, but with a bit of intention and focus, you can quickly assemble and mine it to begin the segmentation process. You might also consider conducting additional surveys to collect need-based customer preferences, but beginning with the data you already have is a good first step. Figure 8.2 lists some of the data that are typically readily available in any organization.

The primary objective of segmentation through data analytics is to identify the profile of your most successful and profitable existing customers. Your sales force employees might think they know who these customers are, but chances are they're mostly relying on intuition and experience. By adding the data-analytics dimension to the identification process, you can validate some of these impressions and accelerate the process. The next step is to

Selling Without Segmentation

1) Splitting time equally among all customers.
2) Favoring the process instead of the content because of the high number of accounts to manage.
3) Visiting price buyers who do not want sales interactions.
4) Not spending enough time with "high value" targets.
5) Trying to introduce high-value innovation products to customers who simply will not pay for them.
6) Conducting marketing activities with accounts who do not care.
7) Potentially chasing the wrong prospects.

Figure 8.1 Selling without segmentation.

Data for Segmentation

1) Transactional Data
   (sales, pricing, volume, rebates, bad debts)
2) Customer Survey Data
   (satisfaction, positioning, demographics, behavioral, preferences)
3) Marketing Data
   (web data, NPS, loyalty scores, market share, share of wallet)
4) Quality Data
   (customer scorecard, reject rate, returns, defect, specifications)
5) Supply Chain Data
   (transportation, forecast accuracy, stock rotation, slow moving)

Figure 8.2 Data for segmentation.

identify similar profiles in the market: that is, customers who used to buy from you but no longer do, and prospects who might have similar characteristics. In this way, you're equipping your sales force members with better sales intelligence so that they can better qualify prospects, find greater revenue opportunities with ideal clients, and focus their time with the customers who have the greatest potential and/or who understand the concepts of value. When lead generation and sales effectiveness increase, you're allocating your efforts at the right time with the most profitable accounts.

Successful segmentation allows for a scientifically based deployment of sales resources that leads to expense optimization with your existing assets. Finally, your marketing and sales efforts will be targeted to the right customers with the right messaging. Guess what? That makes customers happy and their loyalty level increases. So, you get the picture. Segmentation isn't easy, and requires skills and science. When done right, it delivers tremendous benefits for you and your customers.

That's the theory, of course. In practice, there are many possible complications in running data-based customer segmentation: incomplete data, biased data, fragmented data in different formats and languages, sampling errors in customer surveys, inconclusive data analysis, lack of integrated systems, and no pricing data readily available. We could have come up with many other issues, but let's stick with these. In reality, we have data but we're missing a lot of cylinders to get the segmentation engine running. Running cluster analysis for B2B customer segmentation is one of the most complex statistical analyses, along with conjoint analysis.

The books that focus on quantitative customer segmentation omit the fact that a good segmentation analysis begins with a qualitative segmentation process. This is what we call integrative customer segmentation, which includes qualitative segmentation, validated with quantitative segmentation and then tied to transactional data. Integrating the three components allows you to operationalize your segmentation. That works well in the retail world or the B2C sector when you have many customers to research. It's harder to do in the B2B and industrial worlds.

Get the design right to get the execution right

Sometimes a B2B or industrial customer population might only have a dozen global accounts. In some business-to-defense markets, there are just one or two accounts! So what do you do? Give up and not do any segmentation? This is where it gets complicated, and for two reasons. First, go-to-market professionals with engineering and analytical mindsets struggle with the notion of qualitative work. They want hard facts derived from statistics. Second, your customer segmentation may end up having two or three segments with just a few customers in each. That leads to a lack of confidence in the process and a quick return to traditional firmographics or a product-based segmentation process.

Most of the successful B2B customer-segmentation projects we've conducted were done using qualitative information. In general, they were global projects with customer populations ranging from 50 to 200 in B2B or industry-to-industry environments. These qualitative projects took three to six months to complete and required intense deep dives into accounts as well as multiple working sessions with multi-functional groups. It's hard to conduct a qualitative customer-segmentation project without the deep involvement of the sales force and account managers. It isn't going to happen. So, one of the basic rules of engagement is the presence and active support of the commercial teams. Without that, we prefer not to begin such a project. We propose six more best practices for designing and conducting qualitative customer segmentation for superior execution.

1. *Train and experiment in parallel.* Give your team the fundamentals on the topic of segmentation. We usually spend about two hours training on the differences between strategic, market, product, customer, and pricing segmentation. Then we show many examples of how successful companies have done it. The key is to also conduct some easy exercises to get the multi-functional group warmed up. So it's half a day of training and short exercises leading into the first steps of the process.
2. *Focus on information depth.* Because the process is qualitative, we get groups to focus on all customers in the population (prospects, lost accounts, new accounts, legacy accounts, etc.) but also on listing all the potential critical classification criteria that will be used later to segment the customer population in question. It's not unusual to end up with as many as 50 or 60 classification criteria. These criteria focus on firmographics, product purchases, usage of products or services, buying behaviors, nature of the customer organization, customer culture, and more. This exercise typically energizes the working group because they realize that there's much information to capture and later analyze.
3. *Run multiple iterations of the analysis.* Qualitative segmentation requires several iterations with learning in between. The segments that emerge at the end of the first workshop are not what will be used in the end. Although the working group might feel good after the first workshop, more work is needed. The number of iterations will be based on the level of discrimination between the identified segmentations. Are the segments significantly different, or is there too much overlap? Another key question is whether you can put all relevant customers into the buckets you've identified. Remember that in this qualitative process, the sales team is actively involved, so you have to make sure they understand the process and when it is done.
4. *Consider multiple dimensions.* The complexity of qualitative segmentation is that you need to identify discriminant classification criteria qualitatively. A computer isn't doing any statistical testing for significance. You're doing this for the group. Generally, there are three or four such criteria that you can consider at the same time. These criteria come from the list of 50 or 60 criteria you've identified in the initial workshop, as explained in point 2. The reason you must iterate is that you might have to change one or two of these discriminant criteria and start over. Some of the most common B2B discriminant criteria are value/price buyers, service-requirements intensity, technical-maturity level, outsourcing philosophy, and propensity to accept partnership.
5. *Generate trust in the process through validation.* To build adoption of the segmentation process and acceptance of the qualitative process, you need to ensure that the work is validated by the sales force multiple times. As much as 50 percent of your project team will be composed of sellers, and they will represent the entire sales force. One of the projects we conducted had 12 people in the core team, including 6 sales managers from around the world. We then validated the work twice with up to 75 sales representatives using Excel and a short survey. Remember that you have to keep it simple for them. You also need to give them a reason and time to respond.
6. *Rationalize by focusing on the customers, not the process.* Your project team will also include product managers, technical managers and pricing managers who will fight your qualitative process until the last minute! So you need to focus on the customers and not the process. Make sure that the team enters into many exchanges of customer

names, customer data, and examples of customer transactions. You'll get pushback because the process is fuzzy and incomplete. It's not rational enough. If you have 50 customers in your population, make sure you review all of them!

Qualitative customer segmentation works well. But there are many forces that can derail it. One is the desire to test the results of the qualitative work using statistics. We've seen this many times. Some geek proposes to use Excel or another application to mine collected qualitative data so that it can be validated. That's the kiss of death. That doesn't mean that you won't be able to conduct both qualitative and quantitative analyses. We propose that you begin with qualitative and intuitive segmentation and then extend the analytical work by adding the data listed in Figure 8.2 to conduct principal component analysis or cluster analysis. One cannot go without the other. In B2B, the hard work is about gathering deep customer data and identifying the relevant classification criteria. Then the process should continue with both "segment-tuition" and analytical work.

Without being operationalized, customer segmentation is just a theory

We posit that the main issue with customer segmentation relates to the difficulty in operationalizing the outcome of the segmentation analysis. Some teams will work on segmentation and then shelve the PowerPoint deck and the analysis altogether. Customer segmentation is the heart of the marketing-planning process. It comes before the development of your marketing mix, which in turn leads to the commercial execution plan as shown in Figure 8.3. If the first steps of the planning process are skipped, then marketing-mix projects are either one-size-fits-all or focused on product segmentation.

Moving from one type of segmentation approach to another might require putting the organization upside down. And that isn't going to work. So the key is to focus on designing a hybrid segmentation process that takes into account the organizational constraints (regions, legal entity, asset locations) while embracing the go-to-market approach as shown in Figure 8.4. Then you have to be good at executing the whole thing. That means working in a matrix organization pulling resources from various departments and orchestrating customer-segment strategies across departments and functions. This requires a strong discipline of execution with a pinch of change management!

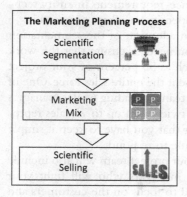

Figure 8.3 The marketing planning process.

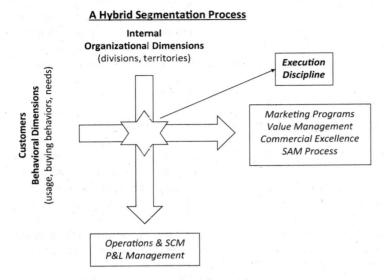

Figure 8.4 A hybrid segmentation process.

Executing your Customer Segmentation

1) Prepare business model and value propositions by customer segment.
2) Prepare a marketing plan by customer segment.
3) Define a modular platform approach across customer segment.
4) Prepare a product and service versioning strategy (good/better/best).
5) Define innovation plans by customer segment.
6) Configure bundle offers for each customer segment.
7) Design pricing/bidding strategy by customer segment.
8) Define commercial approach by customer segment (nature, engagement, intensity, customer support resources).
9) Organize sales, business development, strategic account management functions to engage customer segments holistically.
10) Define resource allocation strategy by segment (HR, Capex, Opex, R&D).

Figure 8.5 Executing your customer segmentation.

You can see the complexity of running and deploying a thorough customer-segmentation process: How do you organize for it? How do you change the internal structure to organize around the customers? Who does what, and who has the authority to allocate funds to customer-segment programs? In Figure 8.5, we propose ten activities that are essential to deploying and executing a customer-segmentation outcome while working within organizational constraints. This list is not exhaustive but focuses on some of the critical go-to-market activities of any organization.

Some of the most successful B2B segmentation projects we've conducted led to the development of business models and marketing plans for each customer segment. In these projects, we had the marketing and sales executives very involved and aligned on what to do next. The team proposed new business models, action plans, and resource plans to the top executives in the business. It was the winning play for the business that was truly customer-focused. These executives had the courage to propose these drastic changes in their go-to-market approach. They had no choice in the end. The market had changed dramatically.

Execute segmentation through scientific selling

Here are some of the critical dimensions of implementing scientific selling:

1. *Revise your sales organizational design.* Growth in sales revenue and in sales expenses can't be considered as a linear relationship. A robust sales-effectiveness assessment will show you how your sales force members are spending their time, where they're spending their time, and what the specific impact of their sales actions are. Mining your sales data will surface areas of dysfunction that can be solved with a new commercial process and a renewed organizational design. Adopting scientific selling based on deep customer segmentation and as part of a commercial-excellence program can give you an amazing opportunity to go through this exercise.
2. *Train your sales force on segmentation and scientific selling.* Change happens. Moving from a traditional sales approach to a scientific segmentation and selling model can represent a potential disruption. Change management and training will become paramount in ensuring that your sales force understands its role, the new commercial process, and the power of data. Don't underestimate the need for communication, training, and reinforcement. Get the sales force onboard as soon as possible.
3. *Grow without increasing your headcount.* Times are still unpredictable. With flat demand curves and growing competitive pressure, sales leadership is asked to do more with less. It's irrational to think that top leadership will give the green light to adding dozens of salespeople to chase growth. The focus should be on sales effectiveness and productivity by focusing on the right and most profitable customer segments. Can you do more and grow with the current headcount level? Can you reallocate your sales force to data-derived market segments to reach your greatest potential? This is what top management will expect to hear from sales leaders.
4. *Beef up your back office.* The role of the back office is critical in the scientific selling model. The back office includes sales operations, lead-generation experts, inside sales teams, and sales-analytics groups. Pricing and IT are also part of the support team. The role of the back-office group is to make sure sales reps are in front of the right customer, at the right time, and with the right data in hand. The end result of this change in paradigm is a reduction of pure sales headcounts and an increase in back-office sales staff.
5. *Reach commercial excellence.* Reaching commercial excellence is not business as usual. Adopting scientific segmentation and selling models requires breakthrough thinking. You can't think of making this change without changing your culture, your organizational design, your support staff, your incentive plans, and so on. It's a transformational exercise that also requires top management training and support.

Optimize your marketing strategy

1. *Marketing resources.* Because your segments will be clearly defined and their needs better understood, your marketing efforts will be better focused to respond to these

needs. In the end, it becomes a matter of the quality of marketing and not the quantity. Moving away from the one-size-fits-all marketing approach will improve your conversion rate and boost the return on investment (ROI) of your marketing investments. In other words, your customers who aren't interested in your glossy brochures or in wearing your latest branded polo shirts shouldn't receive them. That money can be used to better satisfy your core customer target segments.

2. *Customer cost-to-serve.* The combination of cost-to-serve analysis from your pricing analytics solutions and of segmentation will allow you to refine the pricing and service conditions offered to distinct segments. For example, your "value" customers will be offered higher service levels that they are willing to pay for. For your sophisticated technology-driven buyers, a technology-based supply-chain approach might resonate better.
3. *Product mix.* Scientific segmentation allows you to rightsize your product offering to specific market segments. It also allows you to create unique offerings such as product bundles and product-service packages. You might realize, for example, that a large portion of your accounts don't care about the extra performance of your product and aren't willing to pay for it. This may trigger a category-management discussion with research and development (R&D) and marketing that might lead to rightsized products being offered. That implies savings in raw materials, in engineering, and in manufacturing of advanced products and technologies.
4. *Versioning of offerings.* Combine points 1 through 4, and you can imagine the possibilities. Scientific segmentation allows you to version business offerings to respond to specific customer needs. While it might create some complexity, it also allows you to customize your business models to your customer segments. The savings will be immediate!

Whether qualitative or quantitative, customer segmentation generates powerful benefits. So why is the process so neglected in many organizations? The data are there. There's software to help. There are books written on the topic. That's the topic of our fourth consideration.

Recommended guidelines for superior execution

There's no doubt that taking on a deep and dynamic customer-segmentation process and executing the outcome will be a real challenge. In the previous section, we touched on some of the required work and the implied complications. Here are additional guidelines to ensure that you execute successfully.

1. *If you want things to change or get done, manage the resource-allocation process and have someone with authority support budget decisions.* Getting support from top management and having control over marketing budgets are very helpful for the execution part of the process.
2. *Focus on multi-functional design for multi-function execution.* The sooner people participate, the more skin they have in the game. Don't leave any relevant parties out of the process.
3. *Influence strong alignment in the C-suite between key functions.* Make sure sales and marketing are both equally engaged and supportive in the process. Involve the finance and supply-chain executives as well. Internal conflicts and politics will derail the best-designed segmentation project.

4. *Make use of tools (enterprise resource planning [ERP], customer relationship management [CRM], marketing automation, demand generation) to support your business case and to support your implementation projects.* Tools in combination with great design work can be powerful.
5. *Embed customer-segmentation tactics in marketing and sales processes.* The activities listed in Figure 8.5 should be integrated into the marketing and sales process. Behavior changes will happen with the process being implemented.

Conclusion

In times of soul-searching, many businesses will race to cut costs without engaging in deep exploration of their customer-segmentation process. Cost-cutting is a short-term process that rips short-term gains. Scientific qualitative and/or quantitative segmentation can achieve the same optimization of cost and resource allocation, but it also allows you to redesign your firm's offerings and positioning for the long term. Such a scientific exploration can revolutionize a go-to-market strategy while minimizing the incremental costs of better serving your market segments. Segmentation isn't new. It's been around for many decades. It remains one of the most difficult marketing concepts to explore and execute. The considerations we've listed in this chapter might help you get started. To be successful, put the customer first and then adopt an agile and hybrid process. Not the other way around. Then focus on execution. Too many customer-segmentation projects end up shelved or kept in very static documents. Design your customer segmentation with execution in mind.

9 Training programs to boost pricing execution

Stephan M. Liozu

The development of people skills through a thorough training plan is essential to proper pricing execution. Generally speaking, whether we're discussing the deployment of a tool, the assimilation of a new pricing method, or a large-scale pricing-execution program, pricing training is the engine of the pricing transformation. Training is how we establish a growth mindset in the organization and tap the potential of people when embracing pricing activities. It's how we impart the organization's new vision, objectives, concepts, approaches, and tools to each rank-and-file employee, to each team, and to each executive throughout the business. Your company deserves this investment in dedicated training.

At the same time, how do we distill and pass along best practices for pricing training when every business is different? Differences in scope, culture, and market mean that every pricing training program requires customization. Meeting that challenge isn't easy, but it brings great rewards when you meet or exceed your pricing-implementation targets. You'll have more dedicated, aligned, productive employees who see that you've invested in their futures.

Despite – or perhaps because of – this demand for customized training, following is a list of training best practices that can help you achieve the results your team and organization expect and deserve. These lessons are based on a career of initiating pricing and value transformations, coaching people in organizations across the world, and helping them take advantage of new tools and ideas as well as ones they already have access to.

The goal is to train and retrain, constantly checking in with the individuals to reinstill the values of the hard work done in the original training. Remember that the point of a pricing transformation is to better ourselves and our performance, individually and as an organization.

Step 1: Rethink how pricing training works

Let's be realistic about the scope here. We'll be training many different people on many different things. This cannot occur overnight; nor can it occur using conventional methods. The best-practice model we'll use is instead a total redesign of the traditional lecture-class approach. We have to stop carpet-bombing people with information, then releasing them back to their own devices to sink or swim. Feedback and follow-up are critical.

Instead of relying on day-long lectures or PowerPoint overdose, a formal training session is only the beginning. Training should take place over a period of 3 to 6 or even 12 months, during which we'll collect multiple data points and have multiple contacts with each trainee to reinforce execution and full assimilation of concepts. In reality, training never ends, just as the pricing transformation never ends. The roadmap needs to account for many touch points of reinforcement. New people will come and go in your organization, requiring frequent training blitzes.

Step 2: Plan and create a roadmap

Over time and on a regular schedule, the trainer must touch base with the trainees. To ensure that you stay on schedule, first design a rough draft with a timeline for your training. Then create a list of touch points based on the deployment and execution plan. Before you attempt to merge these tools into a roadmap, create a template or a document for this roadmap in simple spreadsheet software. List the weeks along the top and the touch points along the side.

To come up with the time plan, begin by listing things like in-house obligations that can help you define available time. You'll need to account for webinars, monthly meetings, weekly sales calls, email blasts, text campaign, daily reminders, and so forth. With these in mind, you can map out when the training (and the transformation steps) can actually occur. This will help you set a timeline for how long it will take and what formats you might follow.

The touch points for follow-up will reinforce the initial pricing training content. The number of touch points is important: the more, the better. You're not trying to minimize or optimize the number of touch points right now. The objective is to make the content stick. Saturation and the constant backing up of this knowledge are crucial. The recommendation is to have ten touch points with each trainee in a space of three to six weeks after the original presentation of material. This is much stronger reinforcement than what you achieve over the span of two hours at a conference or a national sales meeting, for example.

To keep these ten touch points from becoming a monotonous burden, you should include a mix of delivery methods in your roadmap, including virtual and in-person methods as well as hybrid forms. Watch a video in a classroom, then get out of your seats and complete an exercise based on the information presented. You may also have multiple trainers connecting to a single platform, using their different coaching skills at a single point. Maybe you can use something as simple as a phone call plus matching video. No matter how you perform the task, the key to absorption is to engage trainees over the space of three to six months. Use all available technologies at your disposal and be creative. And focus on the critical aspects of your pricing-execution plan. If three or four key pricing tactics need to be changed or introduced, they will be the heart of the training program and will be repeated over and over.

Step 3: Get the blend of methods right

Flexibility is essential to finding the right blend of methods for successful pricing-transformation training. With today's ever-increasing levels of technology and globalization, you can't expect to have all the people you need in a room whenever you need them. In fact, apart from an initial meeting, it may be logistically impossible to get the entire group together again. You have no choice but to find alternative approaches.

We have to diversify and be flexible in our delivery methods. As their pricing coach and leader, you have to touch base with them any way you can and avoid using technology or timing as an excuse. Whatever the method, proper use of time is essential to achieving the maximum number of touch points in the amount of time provided.

Think beyond traditional methods and look for openings in people's schedules. Maybe you take advantage of something as simple as a layover between flights for a quick trainer call. Or you can record podcasts for trainees to listen to while commuting. Take advantage of local team meetings or gatherings to hold peer discussions on value. There are many options to weigh and leverage without waiting for a conventional two-hour meeting next time they are in town or trying to wedge a full-day workshop into people's busy lives.

You also need to vary the style and voice of your follow-ups. This is another reason why we need to have several people involved as leaders, coaches, and trainers. You cannot have the same person giving the entire training over a period of months. People need variety to maintain focus and absorb information. Here you can look to internal options first. There's no reason why every level can't participate, from the CEO down to the trainees' peers.

We're using the available time of all these opinion leaders to ensure that we deliver the messages consistently. You can use an external coach or trainer to deliver the initial message or concept, but the best follow-up is constant reinforcement from within. Include managers, some coaches, executives, value experts, direct supervisors, and peers. Peers should not be just any peers; they should be value leaders themselves, well versed in your value message and ideally having performed a similar task in a previous job. These individuals are perfect for delivering messages and training.

You might be surprised by the number of people in your organization who are already pricing and value experts and who are willing to act as an energizing force to support your execution efforts! In any organization, there are always several people who've received recognition for "best in class" training at some point in their lives. These individuals are everywhere, and their value experience can offer you a massive boost in training other employees. Even better, they are often eager to assist and spread their positive attitude. This is highly valuable when motivating others to commit to a plan and targets. Identifying these individuals early in the planning process is important. Often you only need to ask a few simple direct questions to discover whether anyone has any such experience.

One unbeatable advantage these peers can have is their ability to tell a story about their previous pricing successes. They can share pragmatic pains and gains of their own journey. Storytelling is in vogue as a training approach, and it should be an important form of training in any extensive, broad-based program. The stories these individuals can share of their individual transformation will add a personal touch to the journey. It gives their peers something to identify with and commit to. It gives them hope that it can be done. Hope, in turn, brings confidence to take action. If you have all these value managers eager to share their story, why not use them to your advantage?

Storytelling and training approaches do not always need to come from within, though. To supplement your own pricing and value leaders, you can get creative here as well. Retired executives, professional athletes, coaches, military veterans, and even your own customers and suppliers can add invaluable insights to the content you want to convey, and do so in a way that no classroom teacher ever could.

You can also use online resources and platforms to supplement your own approaches and stories. Online cloud platforms can encourage ad-hoc interaction, which can be valuable far beyond your planned training. They offer file and slide sharing so that colleagues can interact and offer each other advice and feedback. These platforms can also connect them with their trainers and coaches. We can't capture these touch points in our roadmap in advance, because they're spontaneous and help new internal networks grow organically.

You can also tap into websites with reinforcement training. One such site is Khan Academy, a non-profit educational organization created in 2006 by educator Salaman Khan with the goal of creating an accessible place for people to learn. The organization produces short lectures in the form of YouTube videos on a broad range of topics. The website also includes supplementary practice exercises and tools for educators. This is just one example of a tool that could be set up internally to add extra touch points.

Step 4: Work to help each individual absorb the material

Think about how you might help your kids when they're doing their homework, or how teachers are trained to differentiate between students of varying ability. They must deliver the same subject, the same topic, but must work harder with some students to make sure they absorb the material. They figure out a blend of techniques over time with concepts that resonate best with each individual student. They must make the material relevant and interesting.

Why should the business world be any different?

To get an organization of diverse individuals to absorb and embody the same ideas is challenging, but not impossible. Each individual learns differently, and each may be captivated by different things. They may even have different capacities to process information, sometimes referred to in academia as "absorptive capacity." We want to transform peoples' mindsets and get them into the transformational-change mode. Begin simply and increase complexity over time. You don't want to overwhelm them with too much work. We want to ensure that the knowledge they're getting sticks, and there are proven and universal best practices we can capitalize on. Here's a basic approach to concepts and application:

- *Begin with a 50/50 mix*: in the first wave, present 50 percent exercises and 50 percent concepts. The concepts should be delivered like emails, tips, small items to read, training, and ideas.
- *Aim later for an 80/20 mix*: as you progress in the pricing execution, 80 percent will be exercises and 20 percent will be concepts. This depends on the project, of course!
- *Continue with 100 percent coaching for reinforcement over time, especially focusing on those who are a bit behind*.
- *Keep it relevant*: deliver concepts that are relevant to people's daily work and not theoretical. This is one of the most important filters you have. Focus on your key goals and objectives.
- *Experiment*: one effective exercise is speed role-playing, where you give the audience a little exercise and within five minutes they must role-play it.
- *Play and test*: have the trainees role-play using the pricing tools. These skills will be directly transferrable and critical to reinforce.
- *Help people feel comfortable*: during role-play exercises, no supervisors should be in the room with subordinates. The idea is to create a comfort zone.
- *Have fun*: you can't be serious or intense all the time.

The point of these exercises is to create confidence in the processes, in the new pricing tools, and between colleagues. We even did a stomach-bump competition in one program. We set up a jury and awarded prizes to the winners. This event had nothing to do with value, but it allowed the participants to bond and to relax. You can't expect to keep the trainees serious and under pressure. You want them to want to be there!

Even with this approach, you can still lose your trainees if your priority is to stick to an agenda. You have to be agile and flexible. When leading pricing training and finding that something works well, I adjust the tempo and agenda to encompass more of this successful aspect. If something isn't working, I change the agenda, delay some point, or even cancel a section if necessary. The priority should be more about group flow and collective confidence, and less about sticking to the agenda and trainer's ratings.

At the end of the day, collaboration and cooperation keep interest alive and speed absorption. This applies to the team as well as to the coach with the group. Having that intimacy and that bond is much more important than religiously following an agenda. You're building lasting confidence and a sense of trust. Your agility in setting up these training programs and in modifying them reinforces that you're focused on the trainees and their welfare and progress, not on your agenda. Remember that executing pricing programs requires collective confidence and collective action. Don't leave anyone behind!

Summarizing the training best practices for pricing execution

Let's review the best practices for training to superior pricing execution:

- *Plan on at least ten touch points*: conventional classroom instruction is not sufficient, and face-to-face follow-up is often impractical in our global world. You have to stay connected, the more frequently the better.
- *Mix delivery methods*: transmit your methods virtually, physically, or as a hybrid.
- *Mix up your training environment*: training can occur in a classroom, in the field, at home, or even in the car.
- *Use your pricing and business leaders*: the person reinforcing the message can be a manager, coach, team leader, or peer. Each may have a success story to tell.
- *Account for different absorption levels*: some learn best from seeing; others from reading, doing, listening, or taking actions.
- *Trainers and coaches must energize the troops. Energy and positive levels must be significant and genuine. They should feel exhausted at the end of each day.*

With that said, it is time for our own final touch point for this chapter. The key point from this section is that training is now about delivering knowledge: a vigorous, never-ending exchange among multiple trainees and trainers. Because your goal is to get things done and to execute well, your priority is to increase your team's absorptive capacity. The faster you can get to this point, the greater your pricing-execution level will be. So, it's not about conventional lectures and workshops. Training is a continual commitment, and there's no longer time for excuses.

You'll get out of the pricing-execution plan what you put into it. We're doing a lot of rewiring, not only creating new connections for these individuals but rewiring their brains to make sure they have the confidence and the will to execute what we want them to do. We're systemically altering belief systems and instilling a mindset based on growth. We're building their confidence and giving them a platform for success. Success stories are essential, from peers, from people who have done it and from the organization's application of its new knowledge, tools, and techniques.

We must all increase the openness of everyone in the organization, urge them to commit, pique their interest, get things done, and sustain the transformation. Getting 100 percent success in pricing execution requires all the things we've touched on in this chapter. It isn't business as usual. You'll need to collaborate with your leadership development team and your learning organization, and add your own touch to make it a differentiated learning plan.

10 Implementing a structured pricing strategy approach

Ingo Hennecke

Introduction

Bayer AG's journey to holistic pricing excellence consisted of many different steps; this chapter focuses on the implementation of Bayer's pricing strategy methodology. The implementation was a substantial success and has had a sustainable positive financial impact. It included – but was not limited to – a change of mindset in the organization, the adaptation of processes, and the development and rollout of supporting pricing tools.

Bayer's pricing strategy for any new product or service has always been defined by the global product manager and then adapted by region and country to the local market environment. A feedback loop ensures that all involved parties are aligned to avoid misunderstandings on the later price positioning.

However, a structured and guided process supported by specific tools was missing. The global pricing team was asked to fill this gap, and began by evaluating the scientific pricing literature and talking with internal and external pricing experts. The target was development of a pricing strategy methodology focused on the elements most important in Bayer's area of business. Less relevant elements were omitted to avoid information overkill. We finally decided on 12 key elements in our strategy: some common, such as pricing method or pricing role, and some company-specific and confidential.

Because this new pricing strategy methodology would change the way that many people worked, the need for supporting change management activities was evident. We evaluated different change management and transformation methodologies and finally decided to work with John P. Kotter's 8-stage process of creating major change (see Figure 10.1). This methodology had been widely used for other change projects at Bayer and gave this pricing project a clear structure.

1. Establishing a sense of urgency

Prices have always been set since our company's inception, and everybody believes themselves to be an expert in pricing. Therefore, the change of existing processes and the introduction of new pricing methodologies and tools had to be explained and justified to get the necessary acceptance in the organization.

To establish a sense of urgency in the organization, we first identified external developments in our key markets and evaluated their possible impact on our future business:

- Generic producers of agrochemicals trying to grow their market share by selling "on price"

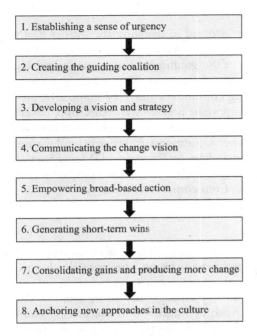

Figure 10.1 The eight-stage process of creating major change.
(*Source*: adapted from Kotter, 1996)

- Low commodity prices for agricultural products reducing customer income and limiting their ability and willingness to pay
- Higher price transparency across countries and regions through internet sites
- Higher market volatility, requiring a more dynamic price strategy
- Ongoing consolidation of customers and channels, leading to higher buying power
- Procurement functions of our customers and channels using more sophisticated methods and tools to challenge our prices

Second, we had to face internal developments, such as cost increases for raw materials, energy and labor, which couldn't be fully compensated for by more efficient production processes. Positioned between price pressure and cost pressure, Bayer needed to capture more value with its products. In particular, our innovations, which provide high customer value, had to contribute more profit if we were to reach our financial targets. This perspective was very much shared and supported by a board member who repeatedly reminded the organization on many occasions that "defining meaningful pricing strategies based on the fair sharing of our offer's customer value will enable us to satisfy our customers with long-term value creation and sustainably achieve our financial targets."

The outcome of the impact evaluation was discussed in many meetings with sales and marketing colleagues from headquarters, regional organizations, and key countries. These discussions created a high awareness of the challenging situation and increased the interest in learning more about the opportunities of a pricing strategy.

2. Creating the guiding coalition

In a global acting company, many functions are involved in bringing the list price of a new product to market. Therefore, every project of this size needs reliable partners to drive the change efficiently and successfully. The core of the guiding coalition was the pricing community, consisting of pricing managers and related functions. Senior management as a sponsor was regularly involved through steering committees and very supportive, providing guidance, advice and budgets. Another important partner was SkillCamp, Bayer's global marketing and sales training platform. Here we were able to spread our content to the countries and receive direct feedback for further adjustments. Another helpful partner was the external part of the pricing community, including the Professional Pricing Society, the European Pricing Platform, and several pricing consultancies. These companies gave us new ideas, helpful tools, and best-practice cases from comparable industries.

3. Developing a vision and strategy

The vision of a mid-sized change project does not necessarily require the broad scope and the resources invested in developing a company group-wide vision. The overarching company vision, however – mentioning, for example, customer centricity and long-term business relationships – set the frame, and all contradictory messages had to be avoided. The vision for pricing was phrased in collaboration with colleagues from the pricing community: "Defining meaningful pricing strategies based on the fair sharing of our offer's customer value will enable us to satisfy our customers with long-term value creation and sustainably achieve our financial targets."

This vision gave our colleagues a clear direction by linking the pricing strategy to the customer value, for example, by balancing the optimization of our customer's business with our own financial targets.

Introducing the "value language"

One important element of our strategy was to introduce a common "value language." In the past there were often misunderstandings about the term "customer value"; for instance, product features and attributes were declared inaccurately as benefits justifying a price premium. In cooperation with our marketing communications team, we therefore enriched the traditional brand benefit ladder (BBL) with the customer value elements (see Figure 10.2). The objective was to show that benefits are not the final outcome but an intermediate step in identifying customer value.

Additionally, we defined a customer benefit as a product feature meeting a customer need and customer value (e.g., economic value) as a quantified benefit. We used these definitions to correct communication documents and challenge statements of colleagues.

4. Communicating the change vision

The best vision is useless if nobody knows or understands it. Therefore, we invested great effort in communicating the vision statement and the supporting elements of the pricing strategy approach. We had to inspire different stakeholder groups and used adequate communication formats to address them in the best way. The three most effective ones were participation in department meetings, the pricing community, and regular newsletters.

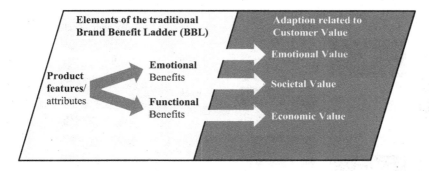

Figure 10.2 The adapted brand benefit ladder.

Department meetings and working sessions. With the support of our sponsors from senior management, we were regularly invited to the monthly meetings of all relevant departments. This allowed us to present the purpose and the progress of the project and to receive constructive feedback. As a follow-up activity, we established one-on-one meetings with all product managers to learn about their current pricing challenges and to discuss future activities. Although this required a time investment of more than ten working days, it fully paid off, as we were able to encourage our colleagues to change their current way of working.

Pricing community. The pricing community consists of global, regional, and local pricing managers as well as selected members from finance, marketing, IT, and internal consulting. The members of this community – in total up to 70 – were eager to act as ambassadors to promote and support the implementation.

Newsletter. Although there appears to be an inflation of change newsletters in our company, they remain an excellent communication channel. A key challenge is to quickly grasp the attention of recipients and enable them to learn as much as possible about the important topics to be addressed. We soon realized that the best lead stories are information about colleagues, best practices from other industries, and interviews with top management, and so we embedded the change information in these formats.

5. Empowering broad-based action

The broad-based action was empowered by increasing the capabilities of the organization. The main focus was on two activities: pricing trainings and pricing tools.

Pricing trainings

Different formats of pricing trainings were developed and offered to the target group of colleagues from marketing, sales, and related functions like finance and controlling. The formats can be differentiated according to the objective of the training: whether to inform, practice, or use.

Inform. This format covers new processes, guidelines, best practices, and examples from other countries. The content can be explained in 2 hours, and open questions can be answered during a short FAQ session afterward. This format is often organized as an online

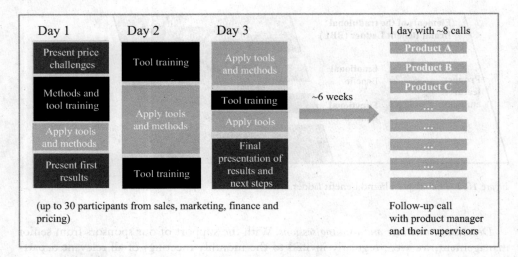

Figure 10.3 Typical workshop setup for key countries.

webinar and offered several times according to different time zones. The webinars are recorded and therefore available for all colleagues on SkillCamp Online, Bayer's training platform. The target group was all colleagues interested in pricing.

Practice. New tools are presented and an exercise is done by using "dummy data" to practice using the tool. This format is easy to set up and rather cost-efficient and scalable; however, the participants – mainly marketing managers – sometimes miss the relationship to their own products, and transfer to daily work life is more difficult.

Use (and transfer). The most successful training format by far is to work on existing challenges with real data and apply the new methodologies (see Figure 10.3). This could be, for example, a three-day workshop using value-pricing methodologies to support a product launch. The participants get a real benefit from this session and can smoothly integrate their new skills into their daily work afterward. An important element of this training format was an individual follow-up call approximately six weeks later. In these calls the global pricing team and the local crop and product managers discussed the progress of every strategy implementation and agreed on next steps.

However, this format – albeit very successful – must be customized to each session and therefore requires significant preparation.

Additionally, a number of pricing topics were included in all relevant marketing and finance training formats – both face-to-face and online. These topics covered, for example, pricing strategy, legal aspects of pricing, value quantification and sharing, and commercial policies. The sessions lasted up to two hours, and the main purpose was to create awareness among the participants and evaluate the need for and interest in a more specific and advanced training.

Pricing tools

In the area of pricing strategy, two important tools were introduced to support the new processes and methodologies.

Strategy tool: a web-based tool to support the set up and sharing of a pricing strategy

The structure of our pricing strategy was developed by the pricing team in collaboration with relevant functions and contains all relevant information and decisions taken. In total, 12 key elements are covered. The first version was a PowerPoint template to test the strategy's acceptance and user-friendliness. The feedback from regions and countries was integrated and led to improvements in content and format. The obvious next step was to move to a web-based platform to further optimize the user experience and facilitate storage. We decided to inspire an active exchange among different countries by giving all users read-only access to existing strategies.

Key objectives of the pricing strategy tool were to:

- Facilitate the alignment and exchange between global, regions, and countries
- Give direction for the price implementation and execution
- Document key assumptions and decisions

LeveragePoint®: one of the most used value management tools at Bayer

This tool is used mainly to set up value models identifying and calculating the differential value of our offers. LeveragePoint replaced a rather simple customer value calculator in Excel that had been used only on a very basic level in the organization. LeveragePoint's intuitive handling and spectrum of additional useful functionalities strongly supported the change to a more value-based mindset in our organization.

6. Generating short-term wins

Nobody wants to be the first to try something new that might fail. Therefore, the best promotion for change is a great success story in a comparable market to show that "it works – and it works great!"

Unfortunately, Bayer's products have a development phase of more than ten years, and there is a long period between the first pricing-strategy/value-pricing activities and a measurable financial impact on our sales figures. This is where our pricing community really made the difference. The regional and local pricing managers were so convinced of the new pricing approach that they challenged already agreed-upon prices of products shortly before launch.

In many cases the managers identified additional customer value and implemented price premiums leading to a significant profit increase. These best-practice examples of short-term wins were quantified, documented, and integrated in our trainings and communications. They helped to further convince the other marketing colleagues and gave our senior management hard facts to justify the necessary investments in tools.

7. Consolidating gains and producing more change

In the following two years we rolled out the initiative to additional markets. The regional and local pricing managers in particular did a great job keeping the pressure up and implementing the processes and tools in their countries. The increasing number of success stories and positive experiences spread by word of mouth and resulted in growing interest in changing to the new methodologies. During this period, more than 1,000 colleagues from sales and marketing were trained, and the number of key users for the tools significantly increased.

8. Anchoring new approaches in the culture

Repeating and repeating

The most important activity to anchor this approach was to change the mindset of the colleagues involved by explaining to them their individual advantages: *What's in for me?*

However, other than in theory this couldn't be done with just a single communication, because of the following challenges we faced:

- Competition with many other internal change initiatives
- Fluctuation and internal job rotation of employees

Therefore, a constant repetition of individual meetings, trainings, and other promoting activities was required.

The guideline document

Another element key to anchoring the new approach in the company's culture was the setup of a guideline document – signed by several members of the executive committee and distributed to the entire organization. In the company culture, this kind of document clearly shows the backing of our top management and indicates that a return to former behavioral patterns will not be accepted. The new guideline included a RACI (Responsibility – Accountability – Consulted – Informed) assignment matrix defining which functions must fulfill the necessary tasks. Additionally, it introduced the necessary tools and described their correct usage step by step. In trainings, this document is used as the basis for the local implementation planning; thus, our internal audit team monitors the correct implementation.

Support from internal audit

The internal audit team regularly checks processes and activities specifically in the area of marketing and sales. Among the audit team's activities is to check whether countries have been following the guideline document and have used the right methodologies for their price setting and getting. This has proven to be a very supportive driver of behavior change in country organizations.

External surveys to show the impact

The usage of external surveys ensures that we get information from our customers about how they perceive the value of our innovations in relation to our pricing. Using experienced market research companies, selecting the right sample and applying advanced questioning techniques ensures that the outcome is representative and free from undesirable influences.

We have developed a two-source approach by including the relevant questions in:

- *Customer*-related surveys (e.g., customer satisfaction surveys)
- *Brand*-related surveys (e.g., brand health checks)

This setup provides good insights, which can be used to adjust our pricing strategy where necessary. The disadvantages are the high costs of external surveys. Therefore, this approach is mainly used only for key brands in key markets.

Summary

The journey toward pricing excellence – which Bayer began in 2005 – is long, and although we've made great progress we still have more steps to take. The process of implementing our pricing strategy methodology – including value pricing – described here is an important part of the entire initiative and has changed how our colleagues think about pricing and how they prepare product launches and set prices. Many successful cases have proven the applicability by improving the price positioning and contributing significantly to the profit targets.

Kotter's change management methodology helped us identify and organize the necessary activities in a structured way. All eight stages were important and contributed to the overall achievements; however, having the right team in place was the ultimate success factor.

Reference

Kotter, J. P. (1996) *Leading Change*, Boston, MA: Harvard Business School Press.

Part 5

Implementing pricing strategies that win deals

11 Pricing large deals

Insights into capabilities and tools that help to win large deals profitably

Andreas Hinterhuber

In this chapter I focus on two elements that help business-to-business (B2B) companies increase win rates and prices on large deals: value quantification and mapping of B2B purchase criteria. I first provide some context on pricing and on the role of large deals for B2B companies.

Offer dispersion in B2B: highly concentrated

Offers are typically concentrated in industrial markets. An analysis of the dispersion of offer and of invoice values provides the data: in recent projects with large, global B2B companies, my colleagues and I normally find that 4 to 10 percent of offers account for approximately 80 percent of the total annual offer value. Getting pricing right on the few large deals that truly matter is thus fundamentally important to increasing overall firm performance.

Pricing: the most important, but frequently most neglected, profit driver

Pricing has a strong, but frequently underappreciated, effect on profits. A study of a sample of Fortune 500 companies suggests that the impact of pricing on profitability by far exceeds the impact of other elements of the marketing mix (Hinterhuber 2004). An increase in average selling prices of 5 percent increases earnings before interest and taxes (EBIT) by 22 percent on average, while other activities, such as revenue growth or cost reduction, have a much smaller impact (see Figure 11.1).

Pricing is an important contributor to company profits. It is frequently neglected, left in the hands of sales or account managers who lack the capabilities, tools, and incentives required for profitable pricing.

Value quantification and the mapping of B2B purchase criteria are activities that help sales and account managers identify price points that increase the likelihood of profitably winning large deals.

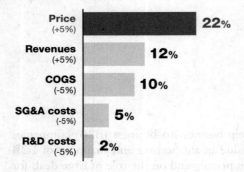

Figure 11.1 Pricing is the key profit driver.

(*Source*: Hinterhuber 2004)

Value quantification: a key requirement for sellers in industrial markets

Buyer expectations of strategic account managers and sales managers are changing (Hinterhuber 2017b, 2017a): in the past, selling was mainly about communicating product benefits and features. This is no longer enough: today, sales and account managers must document and quantify value to customers. A survey of 100 IT buyers at Fortune 1000 firms suggests that 81 percent of buyers expect vendors to quantify the financial value proposition of their solutions (Ernst & Young 2002). Figure 11.2 provides salient insights of this survey.

A subsequent survey asked 600 IT buyers about major shortcomings in their suppliers' sales and marketing organizations (McMurchy 2008). These buyers see an inability to

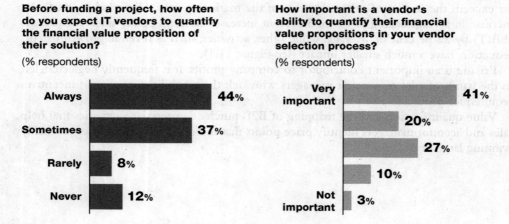

Figure 11.2 Customers expect sales managers to quantify value.

(*Source*: adapted from Ernst & Young 2002)

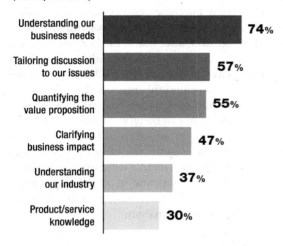

Figure 11.3 Most sales and marketing managers lack value quantification skills.
(*Source*: adapted from McMurchy 2008)

quantify the value proposition and an inability to clarify its business impact as important supplier weaknesses (see Figure 11.3).

These surveys suggest the following. First, sellers in industrial markets are expected to quantify value. Second, B2B buyers do not perceive that sellers are especially proficient in value quantification. This leads to the question of whether value quantification is beneficial in industrial markets: do companies with superior value-quantification capabilities outperform their peers?

A recent empirical survey provides a clear answer: the value-quantification capability, that is, the ability of sales and account managers to translate a firm's competitive advantages into quantified, monetary customer benefits, strongly improves firm performance (Hinterhuber 2017b). Developing value-quantification capabilities is thus a key differentiator for high-performing sales organizations.

Value quantification in practice

What is value quantification? It's the ability to translate a firm's competitive advantages into quantified, monetary customer benefits (Hinterhuber 2017b). Doing so requires translating both quantitative customer benefits (such as revenue/gross margin increases, cost reductions, risk reductions, and capital savings) and qualitative customer benefits (such as ease of doing business, customer relationships, industry experience, brand value, emotional benefits, or other process benefits) into one monetary value equating total customer benefits received (Hinterhuber 2017b). White papers or quantified business cases are tools that leading B2B companies, including SKF, SAP, GE, Schneider Electric, Maersk, GE, Dell, Rockwell, and 3M, use to quantify the value delivered to customers. I next provide a sanitized case study of a recent consulting project of Hinterhuber & Partners.

For a client in the intelligent traffic systems (ITS) industry, my colleagues and I quantified the financial value of intelligent, connected traffic-display systems to system integrators – companies that purchase these and other products, bundle them with complementary products, and sell a complete solution to city councils or highway operators. We interviewed procurement managers to determine purchase criteria, we collected data from third parties on the performance of competitive traffic-display systems, we conducted workshops to validate preliminary findings, and, after some further research, we were able to determine the performance implications of the competitive advantages of our client's solution for their customers' profitability. Two key factors emerged that accounted for over 80 percent of the total quantified customer value: this process thus turned an initial long list of potential competitive advantages into two factors that sales, marketing, and account managers could focus on to convey the financial benefits of their solution to B2B procurement managers.

We used our proprietary Value Quantification Tool to quantify the value of these differentiating factors. We discovered that our client's product delivered a substantial amount of value vis-à-vis competitive solutions. This allowed us to determine, in a next step, a price that would allow our client sustained profitability and the client's customers an attractive return on investment. Figure 11.4 provides the result of this analysis.

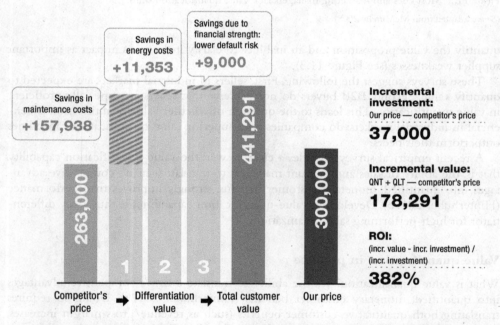

The product of the client company has a price premium of about 14% vis-à-vis the customer's best available alternative: 300k € vs 263 k €. The quantification of customer benefits shows that the customer benefits exceed the price premium by a factor of 4, mainly driven by savings in maintenance.

Figure 11.4 Value quantification – key to justify price premiums.

(*Source*: Hinterhuber & Partners 2016)

As a result of the process of value quantification, the price premium of the company's product loses its negative connotation. The price premium of 14 percent is actually small compared with the return on investment of about 380 percent for customers purchasing the connected, intelligent traffic-display systems.

Value quantification is therefore an important process that allows procurement managers to put price in perspective: it relates price differences to differences in monetary, customer-specific value. There's a catch: since value quantification determines total quantified customer benefits, it identifies just the upper boundary of selling prices; it cannot recommend a specific, profit-optimizing, selling price (Nagle et al. 2011). The process of value quantification thus leaves it to sellers to identify specific deal prices by taking into consideration other factors such as company goals (revenue vs. profit maximization), customer price sensitivity, relative power vis-à-vis purchasers, competitive intensity, and customer price perceptions. The fact that value quantification provides a range of prices instead of recommending a specific, profit-maximizing price point is usually not a limitation in those instances where sellers have the possibility of negotiating prices. Prices are adjusted in the negotiation based on new information: information on the weight of price vis-à-vis other criteria or information on competitor price levels or product features. In a negotiated setting, the process of value quantification can therefore help to win the deal by providing buyers compelling arguments on the business case of one supplier vis-à-vis a variety of other suppliers with apparently lower prices.

In competitive bidding situations, there is usually no chance to renegotiate prices. There's one shot to get pricing right. The process of value quantification needs to be complemented with data on competitive offerings and data on customer purchase criteria. Two of the most prominent approaches providing these insights are B2B purchase-criteria mapping and bid-response functions. In this chapter I focus on B2B purchase-criteria mapping; on bid-response functions, see Phillips (2005).

Mapping B2B purchase criteria

Sales managers typically have an important weakness: "They do not listen," says Bernard Quancard, CEO of the Strategic Account Management Association (Hinterhuber et al. 2017: 44). Numerous empirical studies confirm that B2B buyers perceive their sales managers as lacking in listening skills: understanding client business needs is the most important shortcoming that IT buyers mention about sellers in the study cited earlier (see Figure 11.3). An earlier study similarly finds that a top complaint about sales managers is that they "do not listen" (HR Chally Group 2002).

Mapping B2B purchase criteria is a systematic process that aims to understand the importance and weight of B2B customer purchase criteria and the relative performance of alternative suppliers on these criteria in order to determine a selling price that maximizes the chances of winning the deal. Mapping B2B purchase criteria of course requires understanding them in the first place. One way to map B2B purchase criteria is to use a matrix that B2B procurement organizations frequently use to evaluate alternative suppliers. Figure 11.5 provides an example.

This matrix requires two main inputs. First is an understanding of B2B customer purchase criteria. Sales and account managers should rank and weigh these criteria: for public

The initial proposal of senior management was to price substantially below expected price levels of competitors in order to win.

Criterion	Weight	Performance Hinterhuber & Partners client	Performance Competitor A	Performance Competitor B
Facilities: space, decor, layout	30%	4	3	4
Price	25%	5	4	3
Accesibility	20%	2	4	4
Ease of doing business: speed, proposal quality	15%	5	3	3
Track record, credibility	10%	3	3	3
Total:	**100%**	**3,9**	**3,5**	**3,5**

Rating on 1-5 scale, 5 is best rating
For price: 5 is lowest price

Hinterhuber & Partners client
- Facilities + ☺
- Price + ☺
- Accesibility − ☹
- Ease of bus + ☺
- Track record = 😐

● H&P client: **lowest price**

Figure 11.5 Mapping of B2B purchase criteria: pricing low to increase win rates.
(*Source*: Hinterhuber & Partners 2016)

tenders the criteria are, this is clear, published. Second is insights into their own performance and the performance of key competitors on these purchase criteria. Sales managers should measure the performance of their own company and the performance of two or three key competitors on the purchase criteria. They should of course take the perspective of the specific procurement organization that is evaluating the bid. Data sources are customer interviews, customer surveys, or third-party data on performance in actual field conditions.

The example, also from a recent consulting project of Hinterhuber & Partners, illustrates how our client initially attempted to win the bid. Client management at first suggested bidding below key competitors in order to achieve the highest score on the supplier evaluation matrix.

Our research helped the client win the deal at a price premium vis-à-vis the main competitor. The research uncovered purchase criteria first. We then measured customer-perceived performance and objective performance against these criteria. We also identified ways to further differentiate the client's offering from those of key competitors along the most important purchase criteria (see Figure 11.6 for details). The research provided insights into unmet customer needs that helped differentiate the product and create a truly distinctive offer. Mapping of purchase criteria on the matrix led to the conclusion that the client had a reasonably high chance of winning the bid at a premium price vis-à-vis the main competitor. This turned out to be the case.

As a result of the research by Hinterhuber & Partners on purchase criteria, the client company improved the product, increased the price and won the bid — despite a substantial price premium vis-a-vis the main competitor.

Criterion	Weight	Performance Hinterhuber & Partners client	Performance Competitor A	Performance Competitor B
Facilities: space, decor, layout	30%	5	3	4
Price	25%	3	4	3
Accesibility	20%	2	4	4
Ease of doing business: speed, proposal quality	15%	5	3	3
Track record, credibility	10%	3	3	3
Total:	**100%**	**3,7**	**3,5**	**3,5**

Rating on 1-5 scale, 5 is best rating
For price: 5 is lowest price

Hinterhuber & Partners client
Facilities   + 😊
Price   = ☹
Accesibility − ☹
Ease of bus + 😊
Track record = 😐

H&P client: premium price vis-a-vis main competitor

Figure 11.6 Mapping of key purchase criteria: improving differentiation to win bids at premium prices.
(*Source*: Hinterhuber & Partners 2016)

Putting the idea into practice

Pricing has an immediate, substantial impact on profitability. Pricing isn't easy. Pricing that is too low leads to low profits, pricing that is too high leads to low revenues. The pricing sweet spot is thus low enough to win the deal and high enough to do so profitably.

In simple terms, this article highlights the importance of one key factor in winning large deals profitably: preparation. Preparation wins deals, as opposed to an escalation involving ever-more-senior management levels depending on deal size. Value quantification translates competitive advantages into customer-specific economic benefits and thus identifies the upper boundary of selling prices. B2B purchase-criteria mapping plugs a specific, profit-optimizing selling price into a matrix comparing the overall attractiveness of alternative offers in order to understand the likelihood of winning the deal at any given price.

Winning the next big deal profitably is the ambition of every sales manager, every account manager, and every CEO. Big deals are few: value quantification and B2B purchase-criteria mapping can help identify the sweet spot of pricing that identifies profitable price points that win the next big deal.

Acknowledgments

This article is reprinted with permission from Hinterhuber, A., Pricing large deals, *Velocity*, 21(1), 2019, the magazine of the Strategic Account Management Association.

References

Ernst & Young (2002) "Fortune 1000 IT Buyer Survey: What could shorten sales cycles and further increase win rates for technology vendors?" Economics & Business Analytics white paper.

Hinterhuber, A. (2004) "Towards value-based pricing – an integrative framework for decision making," *Industrial Marketing Management* 33(8): 765–78.

Hinterhuber, A. (2017a) "Value quantification – processes and best practices to document and quantify value in B2B," in: Hinterhuber, A. and Snelgrove, T. (eds.) *Value First, then Price: Quantifying Value in Business Markets from the Perspective of Both Buyers and Sellers*, pp. 61–74, Milton Park, UK: Routledge.

Hinterhuber, A. (2017b) "Value quantification capabilities in industrial markets", *Journal of Business Research* 76: 163–78.

Hinterhuber & Partners (2016) "Best practices in quantified value propositions." White paper, Innsbruck, Austria.

Hinterhuber, A., Snelgrove, T. and Quancard, B. (2017) "Interview: Nurturing value quantification capabilities in strategic account managers," in: Hinterhuber, A. and Snelgrove, T. (eds.) *Value First, then Price: Quantifying Value in Business Markets from the Perspective of Both Buyers and Sellers*, pp. 39–48, Milton Park, UK: Routledge.

HR Chally Group (2002) *Ten Year Research Report*, Dayton, OH.

McMurchy, N. (2008) "Tough times in IT: How do you exploit the opportunities?" Gartner presentation. 1 December, Stamford, CT.

Nagle, T., Hogan, J. and Zale, J. (2011) *The Strategy and Tactics of Pricing: A Guide to Growing More Profitably*, Upper Saddle River, NJ: Prentice Hall.

Phillips, R. (2005) *Pricing and Revenue Optimization*, Stanford, CA: Stanford University Press.

12 Pricing to win

A framework for strategic bid decision-making

Gerhard Riehl

Introduction

The acquisition of profitable new business in a global campaign environment, such as for aircraft and aircraft services procurement, is extremely challenging. Such campaigns are characterized by the small number of campaigns tendered regularly, the significant cost of participating, and the very long duration of the procurement process until the final contract is awarded. Further, these campaigns are highly complex because of the complexity of the systems and services themselves, the large number and great diversity of stakeholders involved, and the dynamic brought in through different contenders, resulting in a high level of uncertainty in the probability of winning.

Yet, the motivation and pressure on companies to engage are high in such businesses to sustain and grow their market share, workforce, production lines, state-of-the-art technologies and accordingly to safeguard their companies' success. Especially in flat or declining markets or segments, companies are forced to participate and maneuver in unclear and difficult bidding environments.

Finally, the winner takes all and the stakes are extremely high, as the volume of business transactions usually results in multibillion-euro contracts. To master such an environment, companies must gain situational awareness. Clarity and transparency about the probability of winning is required to enable efficient company investment decisions.

In particular, a realistic assessment of the current bid positioning in relation to the competition is important. This forms the basis for an effective bid-strategy development and implementation based on educated, strategic business decision-making. A systematic and structured approach is required to provide a framework, process, and methodology and thus to act successfully in a complex bidding environment. Pricing to Win provides a powerful and proven tool for that.

Pricing to Win: a framework for strategic decision making

Pricing to Win refers to both the process of pricing and the result of a particular bidding decision. It involves choices about the prices, costs, and project scope to win bids at the highest possible price (Newman, 2017). Pricing to Win is a best-practice approach that enables your company to position itself to achieve your business goals. Pricing to Win will improve a company's capabilities to handle challenging campaigns, enable strategic bid decisions, and respectively improve and provide clarity on the probability of winning.

Following a four-step approach to master the bidding challenge

The Pricing to Win framework, process, and method as described here is an end-to-end best-practice approach. It is based on a decade of extensive complex global campaign

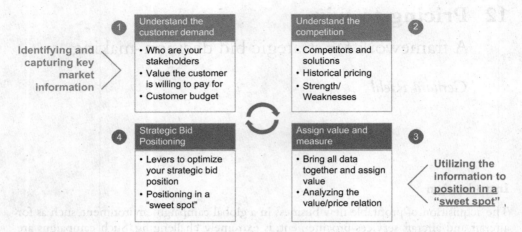

Figure 12.1 This four-step Pricing to Win approach provides a best-practice approach for complex global campaign bidding.

bidding experiences and implements a broad range of lessons learned, gathered from successful as well as from lost campaigns. The Pricing to Win method is clustered in four different steps to simplify its understanding and application.

Steps 1 and 2 of the framework focus on identifying and capturing key customer and market information and requirements, as well as on striving to gain information from the competitors' side. It is further dedicated to translating key stakeholder requirements into a tangible customer value proposition as a baseline for subsequent steps.

Steps 3 and 4 are dedicated to structuring and quantifying the insights and information gathered from the customer and competitor side.

This method further enables you to understand your current relative bid position through visualization and to support the evaluation of key levers for improvement and occupation of your bid position. The intent is to provide a pragmatic, step-by-step approach that can be used in your daily business in support of mastering your bidding challenge (see Figure 12.1).

Step 1: Understand customer demand

Customer demand is triggered by the stakeholders involved. Respectively, the stakeholder requirements and benefits sought for as well as the budget available for procurement are important to be understood.

Who are your stakeholders?

Understanding stakeholders involves understanding stakeholder perception of value. Hinterhuber & Partners states: "Value is always defined by customers and their success metrics. Value is thus subjective, customer-specific, relative, and contextual" (Hinterhuber, 2017: 64).

Business-to-business (B2B) transactions typically involve large and diverse numbers of stakeholders in the procurement and tendering phase.

Typically, some stakeholders' groups are officially involved in a dedicated role as part of the formal tendering process, such as

- the users of the products and services, who usually have the role of describing their requirements and evaluating whether the offers will satisfy their demand;
- a professional procurement organization that drives the tendering process, requests information and clarification from contenders, and prepares reports for the final procurement decision makers;
- research institutions and expert groups asked to provide analysis, compare solutions with each other, and prepare reports on complex subjects; and
- decision makers responsible for supervising the tendering process and making the final sourcing decision.

Additional stakeholder groups include those who do not officially take part in the tendering process, yet who exert their interest and influence on the tendering process, such as

- trade unions, generally interested in the economic benefits and job creation related to the procurement decision, representing their groups of employees;
- lobbying parties representing their specific interests; and
- the public, who are interested in, for example, environmental factors, security issues, and whether taxpayer money will be spent.

The key stakeholders are the people who have direct influence over and authority for final the selection and purchasing decision. Typically, each group of stakeholders will influence the purchasing decisions within the context of their different roles and interests. Therefore, identifying the most important/influential stakeholders is essential to sketching out their value proposition.

Value the customer is willing to pay for

In the Pricing to Win method, value represents one of the two dimensions required to establish a value–price relationship.

Value the customer is willing to pay for always needs to be created with the customer, respectively with their key stakeholders. Therefore, for complex bids, value needs to be sketched out for each influential group of stakeholders involved. Value is related to the solution and benefit that the customer is seeking through the procurement of a system, product, or service. However, how value is perceived and evaluated by the customer will very much depend on the individual's focus and his or her role within the customer organization. As also shown later in the Step 3 graph, a pilot, for example, is more likely to value an aircraft's operational capability more than the national economic benefit such a purchase would bring to a country, whereas a trade union representative may be more likely to value the number of local jobs that would be created by the purchase more than the aircraft's operational capability.

As the *sum of tangible/quantitative and intangible/qualitative aspects*, value becomes multifaceted and multidimensional. To make such an environment tangible and workable, a value proposition needs to be designed, visualized, and tested.

A useful tool for this is the value proposition canvas (Osterwalder and Pigneur, 2010), as it focuses on the customer's profile as well as on the solution offered.

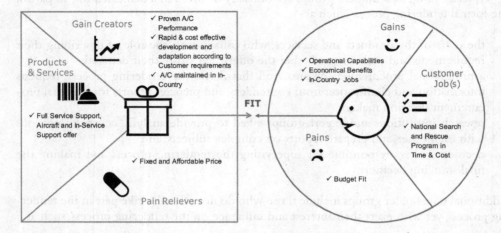

Figure 12.2 A value proposition summary of all different key stakeholder groups forms the baseline for subsequent value quantification and strategic bid positioning.

In a B2B environment, generally a value proposition needs to be established for each group of key stakeholders. For further use and application, the individual stakeholder's value propositions need to be compiled, as detailed in Figure 12.2.

The circle on the right side of the figure describes the customer's profile. This is focused on the job your customer needs to get done; pains, which annoy the customer in the course of getting the job done; and gains expected, which measure the success if the job will be done.

The square on the left side of the figure describes the solution offered. This value map lists all the products and services you offer on which your value proposition builds. Further, it describes how your products and services will relieve the pains, and outlines how the gains are created for the customer.

In Figure 12.2, "fit" refers to whether a match can be achieved between what matters to the customer and the products, features, and services your offer to ease the customer's pains and create gains. A fit between both sides is the key to success.

Customer budget

In the Pricing to Win method, the price, respectively the budget, represents the other dimension required for establishing a value–price relationship.

In B2B transactions the customer's budget is an expression of the money available to be spent for procurement. Respectively, the budget represents the maximum acceptable price from the customer's point of view.

Often, once the budget is set, it acts as a price ceiling, limiting the customer's openness to alternative solutions. The budget in B2B transactions is typically determined as an outcome of an administrative and collaborative planning process involving key stakeholders. Once the budget line is set, there is usually little to no flexibility for later increases or changes. If you cannot stay within the customer's budget with your offered price, your probability of winning is generally very low.

Step 2: Understand the competition

To enable comparison of your own bid position with that of your competitors, and to be able to identify potential bid improvement measures, you need a detailed competitor analysis.

Managers need to gather competitive information. They also need to understand the customer's perception of the relationship between price and value of all relevant competitive offers.

Previous tenders provide a good opportunity to gain a detailed understanding of the competitors' solution for their

- product's functionality and key performance criteria;
- support and service solutions;
- global footprint for, for example, maintenance and repair capabilities;
- historical pricing, for example, price for procuring the aircraft including the setup of necessary support infrastructure, price for operating the aircraft (usually described as a price per flight hour); and
- typical strengths and weaknesses.

Further, it is important to understand the contender's typical competitive behavior and bid strategy. This usually provides insights on the level of risk the company is prepared to take.

You should be aware of the current level of order intake available and the contender's appetite for gaining further business. For example, if a competitor has a low order book, or if their product portfolio is approaching the end of its life cycle, their bid strategy may be more aggressive than usual.

The dynamic of a highly competitive bid environment will only be mastered by collecting detailed competitor information, and analyzing, quantifying, and setting it in relation to your own bid.

Step 3: Assign value and measure

Bring all data together and assign value

To bring all data together and assign value, it is of utmost importance that a robust and detailed understanding of the customer's value proposition has been established as detailed in Step 2. The quality of this information and applicability to the key evaluation criteria determine the accuracy and result of the following steps. Step 3 is dedicated to using information and data gathered in the form of a matrix layout. The main objective is the quantification of value information and structuring along the evaluation criteria.

Structure and quantification enable measurement and comparison of our own bid metrics achieved in comparison with the anticipated competitors' bid metrics, in the light of customer value requirements.

Such an exercise needs to be conducted accurately, using the best knowledge available. It is the nature of the activity that the quantification of qualitative data is not always fully scientific and requires expert subject-matter judgment. Experience shows that the accuracy of the exercise is usually not negatively impacted by that, as the same level of subjectivity is applied throughout the exercise. The company's capabilities to structure and quantify the value proposition captured are recognized as a key success factor (see Figure 12.3).

Bringing all data together and assigning values is the baseline to find a "sweet spot"

	Key Evaluation Criteria	Competitor 1	Competitor 2	OWN Bid	
Customer Value	1.1. Operational Capability	Medium	High	Medium	
	1.2. National Economic Benefit	Medium	High	Medium	
	1.3. In-Country Employment	High	High	High	
	1.4. ...	High	Medium	Medium	Competitive benchmarking shows that Competitor 2 initially achieved the highest score.
	1.5. ...	Medium	Medium	Medium	
	1.6. ...	Medium	Medium	Medium	
Price	2.1 Total Acquisition Price	Low	Medium	High	
		Second	First	Third	

Figure 12.3 A structured and quantified customer value proposition matrix, along key evaluation criteria, enables subsequent visualization and positioning.

Analyzing the value–price relationship

Visualization generally means bringing abstract data and relationships into a graphic or visually comprehensible form (see Figure 12.4). This is a step forward in the Pricing to Win approach, as a simple way to allow arranging and visualizing the customer value and price dimensions in relation to each other.

Figure 12.4 exemplarily describes the current bid positions of three contenders as follows:

- Competitor 1: compliant technical performance; its proximity to the budget ceiling may limit room for improvement.
- Competitor 2: high technical performance; distance from the budget ceiling provides a good bid positioning and room for improvement.
- Your own bid: low but compliant technical performance; distance from the budget ceiling provides room for improvement.

Knowing early in the tendering process where your own and your competitors' bids are positioned is very powerful for subsequent bid improvement to position it in a "sweet spot."

Step 4: Strategic bid positioning

With the initiation of Step 4, we have come much closer to achieve the Pricing to Win objective. With this step we take care of our strategic bid positioning.

Levers to optimize your strategic bid position

Hinterhuber & Partners states: "Value is always based on the differentiation relative to the customer's perceived best available alternative" (Hinterhuber, 2017: 65). This insight guides

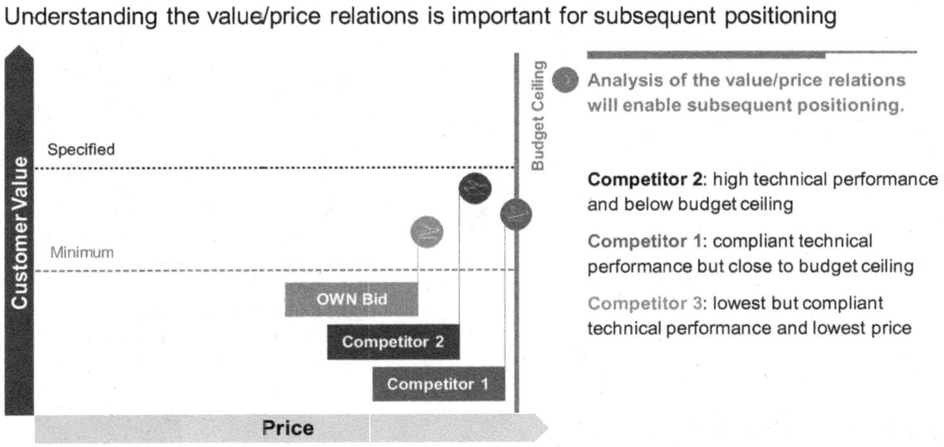

Understanding the value/price relations is important for subsequent positioning

Analysis of the value/price relations will enable subsequent positioning.

Competitor 2: high technical performance and below budget ceiling

Competitor 1: compliant technical performance but close to budget ceiling

Competitor 3: lowest but compliant technical performance and lowest price

Figure 12.4 The customer value–price graph provides a comprehensive overview of your own and your competitors' current bid positions.

the way for identification, evaluation, and selection of the best strategic lever to optimize our bid position.

Based on the already established understanding of current bid positioning as an outcome of Step 3, it is worth thinking about how we can increase and optimize the probability of winning.

To accomplish that, the customer's metrics need to be understood in terms of which economic principle will be applied to measure achievement. This is important to gaining a clear understanding of which direction your bid can improve in. Typically, three different economic principles are applied by customers as benchmarks for achieving their objectives.

The first principle is called *value for money* or the *optimal principle*. This is applied if the customer is seeking the best available relationship between the customer's value and price.

The second economic principle is called the *minimum principle*. This is applied if the customer is seeking the best value at the lowest possible price. In that case, your bid position will improve if the price decrease is higher relative to the customer's value decrease.

The third economic principle is called the *maximum principle*. This is applied if the customer is seeking the highest possible value, exploiting the budget available. In that case, any value increase will improve your bid position if you can stay within the customer's budget. Figure 12.5 illustrates levers for this principle to be applied by the customer.

To achieve the best match between the customer value, requirements, and economic principle applied, different levers need to be considered, allowing the increase or decrease of your value–price relation, such as

- scope, performance, functionality, system availability, quality, and service level;
- delivery schedule, production rate, and ramp-up time;
- liabilities, obligations, and risks; and
- price level.

Strategic levers are important means for positioning in a sweet spot. Levers are usually applied jointly to maximize your improvement initiative.

Figure 12.5 The key levers for optimizing your strategic bid positioning need to be identified, evaluated, and opted for. The graph illustrates the impact of key levers.

Positioning in a sweet spot

The best achievable strategic bid positioning is the sweet spot. Positioning in a sweet spot refers to the development of the maximum preferable bid position, as a sum of identified levers, and in consideration of the customer's economic principle/metrics applied.

The term *sweet spot* also implies that you are the only one who can occupy this competitive position in the customer value–price relation. Even if this sounds a bit high-ambitioned, positioning yourself in the sweet spot is the objective of the Pricing to Win approach described.

Naturally, the room for improvement is limited at some point in any system. To identify the room to maneuver and to provide more clarity about your probability of winning, it is useful to address the limits of the value/price positions. In that sense, the expected limits are important to determine for your own and your competitor's bid position. Also, the customer is limited in their trade space, for example, if the customer value falls below a required threshold or if the price exceeds the budget available.

Figure 12.6 shows a case where the blue-chip contender can position themselves in the sweet spot using the strategic levers identified. Other contenders are not able to follow in that case. This example describes an optimal position for winning the bid.

Let's take a closer look at how we can improve our bid position in our example, resulting in the highest probability of winning. As explained, the customer is seeking the highest possible value, exploiting the budget available maximum principle. Respectively, any value increase will improve our bid position.

The value increase is achieved, first through the provision of additional operational capabilities valued by the customer and second through an increase of in-country employment with procurement of our solution.

In conclusion, with the application of two strategic levers, our customer's value position is the highest among competitors, whereby our price is still within the budget. This bid position provides the highest level of compliance with the customer's expectation, expressed with the maximum principle (see Figure 12.7).

Pricing to win 119

Knowing the trade spaces will enable you to find the "sweet spot"

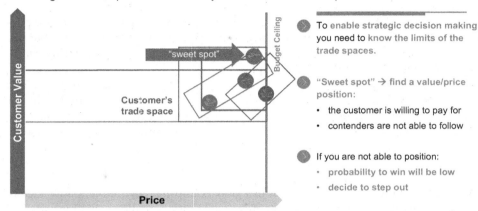

Figure 12.6 Successful strategic bid positioning should consider the customer's, your own, and your competitor's expected trade space as a baseline for decision-making.

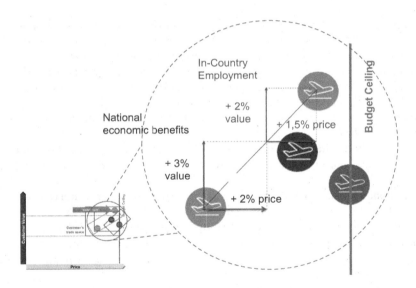

Figure 12.7 Application of two strategic levers, additional operational capabilities and increase of in-country employment, enables optimal best-bid positioning.

For the sake of better understanding, the customers determines what value means, and which economic principle they apply for this metric.

The bid positioning in a maximum/minimum principle environment is mainly focused on the optimization of one dimension, the value or price, as long as we stay within the customer's budget or the customer's mandatory value requirement is not falling short.

For the bid positioning in a value-for-money environment, the focus for optimization is on both dimensions concurrently: value and price. Respectively, the value–price ratio itself plays the key role for determining the most effective strategic levers. Considering that, the positioning in the value-for-money environment is even more challenging, as the best possible combination of value and price may result in a sweet spot.

In case a sweet spot cannot be obtained, a viable alternative is to occupy the best possible trade-off position. This will consequently reduce your probability of winning but still maintain the chance to win. Realistically, your position can be improved during future courses and development of the tendering phases.

Even if a promising position cannot be obtained, an important outcome is also the insight that you will not be able to differentiate. Given this situation, your probability of winning is very low. Of course, this is not in line with the objective to win, but it needs to be understood as a realistic and valuable outcome of our work with a complex system.

Key learnings

The acquisition of profitable new business in a global campaign environment is characterized by a high level of complexity and intensive competition, resulting in a high level of uncertainty in the probability of winning.

The following key learnings have been drawn out of the framework and method described:

1. Situational awareness can be improved by applying a *structured Pricing to Win approach*.
2. Complex bidding usually involves a *diverse group of stakeholders*, each one *influencing the purchasing decision* in the direction of their different roles with their different interests.
3. Mapping of stakeholders and their specific interests enables *identification of the value the customer is willing to pay for*. The *value proposition canvas provides a useful tool*, as it focuses on the customer's profile as well as on the solution offered.
4. A detailed *understanding of the customer's budget is required* to be able to determine the customer's trade-space limit.
5. Competitors are mainly driving the dynamic and increasing the complexity of the bid environment. A *detailed competitor information gathering and analysis is key* to mastering this situation.
6. *Quantification of value information* and structuring along the evaluation criteria *is the critical capability* of the Pricing to Win approach.
7. A graphical *visualization* of the value–price relations *allows simplification of abstract data and their relationships* and enables analysis in a visually comprehensible form.
8. Identification, evaluation, and *selection of strategic levers enable differentiation* relative to the customer's perceived best-available alternative.
9. The economic principle applied by the customer determines the effectiveness of potential strategic levers.
10. A sweet spot is the best achievable strategic bid position, which can only be occupied by you. To identify a sweet spot, you must understand the limits of your own and competitors' trade space.

Thus, the Pricing to Win framework provides you with the situational awareness required for strategic decision-making. Further, it improves your ability to master a complex campaign environment and therefore your probability of winning.

References

Hinterhuber, A. (2017). Value quantification – processes and best practices to document and quantify value in B2B. In A. Hinterhuber and T. Snelgrove (Eds.), *Value First, then Price: Quantifying Value in Business Markets from the Perspective of Both Buyers and Sellers*, pp. 61–74, Milton Park, UK: Routledge.

Newman, L. (2017). *Shipley Proposal Guide*, 4th edition, Kaysville, UT: Shipley Associates.

Osterwalder, A. and Pigneur, Y. (2010). *Business Model Generation: A Handbook for Visionaries, Game Changers, and Challengers*, Hoboken, NJ: John Wiley & Sons.

13 Value quantification

Processes and best practices to document and quantify value in B2B

Andreas Hinterhuber

Introduction

The requirements for a high-performing sales function are changing. In the past, communicating product benefits and features was a key element of sales activities. This is no longer enough. Today, the sales function is increasingly asked to document and quantify value to customers. Consider the results of a survey of 100 IT buyers at Fortune 1000 firms (Ernst & Young 2002): 81 percent expect vendors to quantify the financial value proposition of their solutions (see Figure 13.1).

Similarly, a subsequent survey asked 600 IT buyers about major shortcomings in their suppliers' sales and marketing organizations (McMurchy 2008): IT buyers see an inability

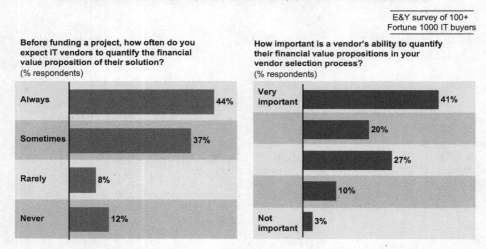

Figure 13.1 Value quantification: a critical requirement in B2B sales.

(*Source*: adapted from Ernst & Young survey of 100+ Fortune 1000 IT buyers; Fortune 1000 IT buyer Survey, Ernst & Young, 2002)

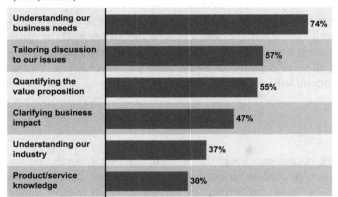

Figure 13.2 Value quantification: a major shortcoming of B2B sellers.

(*Source*: adapted from Gartner survey of 600 IT decision makers of Fortune 2000 companies; Neil McMurchy, Tough Times in IT, Gartner 2009 presentation)

to quantify the value proposition and an inability to clarify its business impact as important supplier weaknesses (see Figure 13.2).

These survey results suggest that the ability to quantify and document the financial impact of the value proposition is critical for sales executives. How well equipped are today's sales managers in this respect? Extant research suggests that business-to-business (B2B) purchasers rate the ability of sales managers to quantify the value proposition as unsatisfactory (Ernst & Young 2002). The conclusion: B2B sales managers must improve their capabilities to quantify and document value.

About the research

Over the last 5 years, my colleagues and I analyzed the value propositions of 125 B2B companies. These companies vary in size and include Fortune 500 companies as well as many small- and medium-sized companies. We complement this research with interviews at dozens of large, and medium-sized companies across a wide range of industries, including automotive, IT services, chemicals, B2B services, pharmaceuticals, forestry, and machinery. In these companies our interlocutors are sales directors, pricing managers, senior executives, and first-level sales managers. Our aim is, first, to collect global best practices in quantified value propositions and, second, to gain insight into the processes that guide the effective development and implementation of quantified value propositions. As a result of this research, I present in the following a framework for the effective development of quantified value propositions. I also present selected case studies that – based on this research – are current global best practices.

The process

Value quantification requires a process. Based on the research, within high-performing sales organizations this process includes the following steps (see Figure 13.3).

To be clear: in some organizations, the process leading to a quantified value proposition is more complex than the steps outlined next. In other companies the actual process is much simpler than outlined: well-developed sales force capabilities ensure that the quantification of the value proposition is a routine component in all major sales pitches, done without explicitly performing all steps outlined in every sales call. Nevertheless, we find that all high-performing sales organizations perform the five steps outlined in one way or another.

Customer insight

The first step in this framework is customer insight. Few companies have developed systematic capabilities in this respect. According to our research, companies that master the development of quantified value propositions strive, first and foremost, to achieve leadership in customer insight. A fundamental component of achieving leadership in customer insight is developing the ability to listen to customers. Jeff Immelt, CEO of General Electric, says, "Listening is the single most undervalued and under-developed business skill" (Clegg 2014). Carol Meyrowitz, CEO of TJX, states, "In all our training we emphasize the importance of listening" (Meyrowitz 2014: 47) – even for apparently inward-oriented functions such as corporate purchasing.

Listening is a key requirement that leads to performance improvements at the level of individual sales managers (Drollinger and Comer 2013), but current research, as well as executives of innovative companies, concur that listening to customers does not and

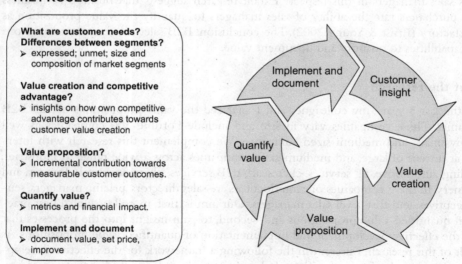

Figure 13.3 The process of value quantification.

cannot imply following customers. The CEOs of Ford, Sony, Apple, and other companies all warn explicitly against taking customer input at face value. Steven Jobs, during his tenure as CEO of NeXT, said,

> It sounds logical to ask customers what they want and then give it to them. ... You can't just ask customers what they want and then try to give that to them. By the time you get it built, they'll want something new.
>
> (Gendron and Burlingham 1989)

Key to generating customer insight is an ability to interpret customers' unmet needs. Two research approaches are noteworthy: ethnographic research and outcome-driven innovation. Ethnographic research is today the gold standard enabling researchers to obtain insight into customers' thought worlds in order to uncover existing, but currently unmet, needs (Cayla, Beers, and Arnould 2014). Ethnographic research is a method borrowed from cultural anthropology that relies on systematic data collection and the systematic recording of human action in natural settings (Arnould and Wallendorf 1994). Participant observation occurs via long-term immersion producing "thick" – richly textured –descriptions (Arnould and Wallendorf 1994: 499). The objective is a credible, not necessarily exhaustive, interpretation of activities aimed at explaining cultural variation. The main data sources are observations in context and verbal reports by participants that frequently and purposefully contain overgeneralizations and idiosyncratic accounts, which researchers interpret. This research method enables researchers to experience the specific, naturally occurring behaviors and conversations of customers in their natural environments. As a result, insight into unsatisfied needs may emerge.

Outcome-driven innovation relies on a combination of qualitative and quantitative research to uncover latent customer needs in order to develop ideas for breakthrough innovations (Hinterhuber 2013).

Create value

The rule is simple: if suppliers are not perceived as being different, then customers will benchmark them on price. The second step in the process of value quantification is thus differentiation along categories that matter to customers. To be clear, differentiation from competitors does not per se add value. It might lead to a sustained investment in product features that add no value for customers. Product differentiation strategies thus have to be preceded by an understanding of the real sources of value for customers (Hinterhuber 2004). Customer insight – step 1 in our process – has to guide differentiation.

The objective of differentiation is to increase customer willingness to pay or total customer value. What is customer value? The definition of customer value in B2B must be based on the following premises of five fundamental principles.

Value is, first, always defined by customers and their success metrics. Value is thus subjective, customer-specific, relative and contextual. Customer insight is the first premise that guides the definition of value. Second: value is always created collaboratively with customers and must be recognized by customers if suppliers expect customers to pay for value. Collaboration is thus the second principle that guides the definition of value. Third: value is the sum of quantitative (financial) and qualitative (intangible) benefits delivered to customers. Value is both hard and soft. Value quantification thus requires that suppliers develop capabilities to quantify the impact of both quantitative and qualitative benefits on key customer success metrics. Quantification of the business impact is thus the third principle that guides the definition of value. Fourth: all value is based on differentiation. Value is always based on the differentiation relative to the customer's perceived best-available alternative. Differentiation is thus the fourth principle that guides the definition of value. Finally: value must be substantiated. For suppliers, value is a promise. For customers, value is an expectation. Suppliers must convert their promises into credible, verifiable and simple deliverables in order to provide customers a realistic assessment of their abilities to deliver the expected results. Figure 13.4 summarizes these fundamental principles that guide the definition of value in B2B.

Customer value is a multifaceted concept; differentiation can thus occur along a number of dimensions. Most important, differentiation is possible also for apparent commodities. Consider the following project, recently completed (Hinterhuber and Pollono 2014).

Executives at a global basic chemical company assume that they are operating in a commodity industry and believe that – in order to achieve meaningful sales – prices for the chemical product in question need to be lowered to the price levels of a low-cost product from China that recently entered the market (indexed at 100 in Figure 13.5). Workshops with executives and focus groups with core customers and distributors allow us to uncover a number of differentiating factors between the low-cost competitor and the company's own offering. Although in no single area do the two products differ dramatically, we find a number of areas where there are small, albeit meaningful, differences between them. Through internal expert estimates and field value-in-use assessments, we quantify customer value for these differentiating features as follows.

We find that small differences in logistical know-how, in product quality, in ordering costs and complexity, in vendor competence, and in customer knowledge add up to a positive differentiation value of 8 percent, thus allowing the company to set prices up to 8 percent above the customer's best alternative. The highest possible price is, of course, not the best price: it leaves no incentive for the customer to purchase. After applying a series

WHAT IS VALUE?

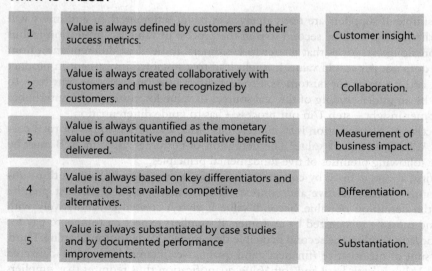

1	Value is always defined by customers and their success metrics.	Customer insight.
2	Value is always created collaboratively with customers and must be recognized by customers.	Collaboration.
3	Value is always quantified as the monetary value of quantitative and qualitative benefits delivered.	Measurement of business impact.
4	Value is always based on key differentiators and relative to best available competitive alternatives.	Differentiation.
5	Value is always substantiated by case studies and by documented performance improvements.	Substantiation.

Figure 13.4 Customer value – basic premises.

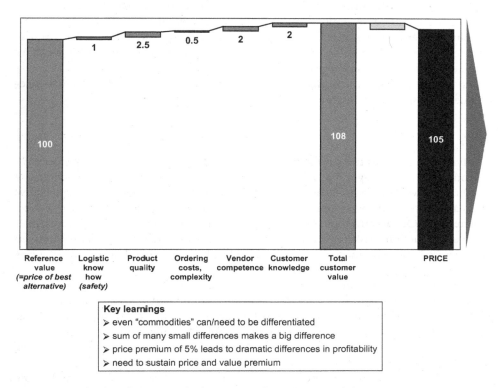

Figure 13.5 Value-based pricing and value creation for B2B commodities.
(*Source*: Hinterhuber & Partners 2016)

of price optimizations, competitive simulations, and estimates of customer reactions, we recommend a final selling price of 105. This represents a price premium of 5 percent over the customer's best available alternative; but this price is, nevertheless, attractive for customers, since their quantified benefits are higher than the price they are expected to pay.

As main learnings of this short case study, we highlight the following points: (a) even apparent commodities can and need to be differentiated, (b) the sum of many small differences in product characteristics can add up to a significant difference in customer value, (c) small price premiums over competitive products (e.g., 5 percent) translate to significant profitability differences between companies, and (d) the price and value premium between two competitive offerings need to be sustained over time via continuous improvement.

Develop the value proposition

The value proposition (Lanning and Michaels 1988) or, alternatively, the value word equation (Anderson, Narus, and Van Rossum 2006), is an instrument designed to translate customer value into quantified, monetary benefits. Anderson et al. (2006: 96) note that "a value word equation expresses … how to assess the differences in functionality or performance between a supplier's offering and the next best alternative and how to convert those differences into dollars." Numerous studies suggest that very few sellers can quantify the value proposition for their customers (Anderson, Kumar and Narus 2007; Hinterhuber 2008). The capability to quantify value is, however, essential. Todd Snelgrove, chief value officer of SKF, states: "Best in class companies have taken the time, effort, and focus to quantify the value of their products and services. If you can't, purchasing will have no choice but to ask for a lower price" (Snelgrove 2013).

Based on our research, I have developed a checklist of elements essential to best-practice value propositions (see Figure 13.6).

Quantify value

Quantifying value means translating competitive advantages into financial customer benefits. Competitive advantages typically deliver either quantitative or qualitative benefits, or both. Quantitative benefits are related exclusively to financial benefits, whereas qualitative benefits are related to process benefits – they allow customers to achieve the same goals in a better way. Quantitative benefits come in four categories: revenue/margin improvements, cost reductions, risk reductions, and capital expense savings. Qualitative benefits include ease of doing business, relationship benefits, knowledge and core competencies, the value of the brand, and other process benefits.

Customer value is the sum of quantitative and qualitative benefits. Value quantification tools visualize the total customer value, that is, the sum of quantitative and qualitative benefits, the price of the company's own product/solution, and the cost of the best-available competitive product. These value quantification tools thus allow return on investment (ROI) calculations: the ROI is the result of relating the price premium to the quantified difference in customer value.

Leading B2B companies routinely perform value quantifications. An example from SKF is illustrated in Figure 13.7 (Hinterhuber and Snelgrove 2012).

BEST PRACTICE VALUE PROPOSITIONS

Check	Item	Key issue	Rate
	Is the target customer group clearly identified?	segment	
	Is the key business issue we resolve a real pain-point for this segment?	relevance	
	Is it clear that the value proposition is superior for this customer group?	better	
	Does the value proposition reflect our competitive advantages?	advantage	
	Is the value proposition relative to the customer's best available alternative?	competition	
	Are customer benefits quantified? Is the quantification the result of quantifying both financial as well as qualitative benefits?	quantify	
	Is the value proposition based on sound customer and market research?	research	
	Does it reflect changing customer priorities? Is it relevant ... tomorrow?	update	
	Can you substantiate the value proposition with case studies or evidence of quantified performance improvements delivered?	substantiate	
	Can you articulate the value proposition in 1-2 minutes?	short	

Figure 13.6 Checklist for developing a best-practice value proposition.

CUSTOMER VALUE-BASED PRICING IN ACTION

Case study
SKF

Price vs. Total Cost — it's about measuring all the factors...

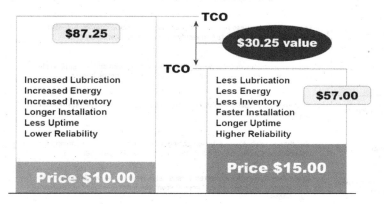

Figure 13.7 Customer value-based pricing in action.
(*Source*: Snelgrove, T., presentation at Strategic Account Management Association, PEC 2016)

Industrial bearings are, for the layperson, commodities: apparently interchangeable steel products used in automotive manufacturing. SKF is able to document to customers that, despite a price premium of 50 percent over the next best-available product, customers end up paying less and being better off by purchasing from SKF.

Marketing, pricing, and sales managers in B2B should take notice: if SKF is able to quantify the value of industrial bearings, so should other companies with products that are frequently even more differentiated than those of SKF.

Implement and document

The final component in the process of value quantification is implementation and documentation of results. The promises outlined in value quantification tools – such as the one in Figure 13.7 – account for nothing unless the value is actually realized in customer operations. In high-performing sales organizations, the following guiding principles underpin this process (see Figure 13.8).

Customer orientation

Customer orientation may appear to be a trite attribute of companies that successfully quantify the value proposition, but it is not. Our research suggests that low-performing sales organizations push their value propositions to customers regardless of whether these value propositions apply in the current context: customer needs may have changed, the next best-available competitive alternative may have changed due to new competitors, the customer's objectives may have changed, or customer capabilities may have shifted. Nothing, our research suggests, destroys the credibility of sales managers quicker than presenting a value proposition to customers without first having gained an in-depth

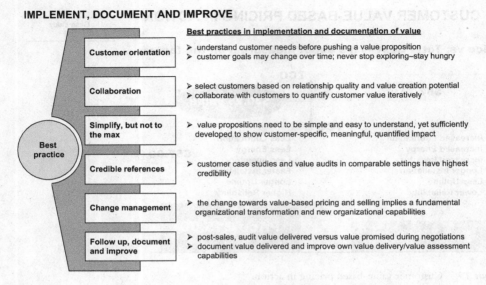

Figure 13.8 Implementing and documenting the quantified value proposition.

understanding of current and future customer needs. The adage "seek first to understand, then to be understood" is also valid in this specific context.

Collaboration

Quantified value propositions are the result of a tight-knit collaboration between vendors and suppliers: credible quantified value propositions cannot be developed in isolation and require that customers give suppliers access to the profit implications of the supplier's offerings for customer operations. This is tricky: in some instances the request for access to customer data highlighting the profit implications of supplier offerings on customer operations can trigger a countervailing request by the customer for access to supplier cost data (Rosenback 2013). This request is reasonable. As a result, negotiated prices for differentiated offerings will settle not between the price of the customer's best-available alternative and total customer value, as the literature on value-based pricing suggests (Nagle and Holden 2002), but between (the likely lower) supplier costs and total customer value.

In this context, customer selection is important: rather than selecting customers based on size or reputation, high-performing sales organizations select customers based on the quality of the relationship and the potential for joint value creation. Furthermore, high-performing sales organizations take time and invest resources to fine-tune the value proposition through multiple iterations, whereas low-performing sales organizations tend to take a hit-or-miss approach. Typically, the latter leads to value propositions that are more generic and less relevant to any particular customer.

Simplify, but not to the maximum

The essence of a quantified value proposition consists of translating the company's competitive advantages into quantified, expected performance improvements. This requires an understanding of competitors and their price and performance level; an understanding of the firm's own competitive advantages; and, finally, an understanding of customers, their needs, and their business models (Hinterhuber 2004). Modeling these relationships is complex: effective value propositions, like all models, are thus always a simplification of reality – but not to the point where simplification leads to meaningless generalization.

Credible references

References enhance the credibility of quantified value propositions. These references can take many forms: summaries of pilot projects, customer case studies, value audits, or documented performance improvements countersigned by customers.

Change management

Institutionalizing value quantification as organizational capability requires organizational change management (Liozu, Hinterhuber, Perelli, and Boland 2012). New approaches to selling, marketing, and pricing frequently require new capabilities, a new organizational structure, different goal and incentive systems, new processes and tools, and new organizational priorities. From an organizational perspective, the implementation of value quantification across the organization must be treated like an ongoing change management process as opposed to a project with a finite life (Hinterhuber and Liozu 2014).

Follow up, document, and improve

As a final element in value quantification, high-performing sales organizations rigorously follow up on actual versus expected quantified value delivered in 6- to 12-month intervals. This enables both customers and suppliers to learn, to analyze causes of performance deviations, and to implement measures to close performance gaps. This documentation also enables suppliers to build a library of documented and quantified performance improvements, by, for example, client function, industry, size, and geographic area. SKF, for example, has built a library containing more than 51,000 case studies of documented and quantified value delivered by SKF, countersigned by customers. This library, SKF's documented solutions program (DSP), is a very powerful selling tool for sales managers when participating in competitive bids with new customers: extant data can be used to estimate likely quantified performance improvements based on a long history of performance improvements in similar situations that customers have actually realized. This documentation is thus an important enabler of organizational learning within suppliers: suppliers learn about typical roadblocks to the realization of expected quantified performance improvements; suppliers also learn about all those areas of their own offering where the realized value is higher than the value they themselves expected to realize. These positive and negative deviations from initial performance expectations are important foundations for gaining an even better, more fine-tuned, and granular understanding of the effect of a firm's own competitive advantages on customer operations. As a result, these deviations will, over time, likely diminish.

Examples of effective quantified value propositions

In the course of our research, we encountered a dozen or so companies that have highly effective quantified value propositions. These well-crafted value propositions support sales and marketing executives during the bidding phase. The ultimate outcomes of effective quantified value propositions are higher prices and higher win rates. As a further benefit, respondents report that the conversation with B2B buying centers shifts: price is less a central concern and the focus shifts toward the quantified performance improvement. Realization of this performance improvement requires that customers and suppliers work together closely. Effective quantified value propositions thus fundamentally change the nature of the customer–supplier relationship, requiring a tight-knit collaborative attitude whereby barriers between the organizations of customers and suppliers start to fall. This ultimately benefits customer satisfaction and customer loyalty.

Recently, Hinterhuber & Partners worked with a global IT service company to define profitable pricing strategies. This company had clear-cut competitive advantages, yet managers struggled to translate these competitive advantages into quantified customer value. As a result, aggressive competitors regularly undercut the company on price. The dilemma was thus: Should the company reduce price in the uncertain hope of gaining volume, or should the company maintain price and risk losing even more revenues?

Hinterhuber & Partners helped this company to escape from these self-imposed limitations. After interviewing managers, customers, distributors; after collecting data on competitive price levels; and after, finally, employing a robust process to identify and quantify key value drivers, we developed a customized value quantification tool that helped the company to understand, precisely, the amount of value a specific product generated for a specific customer segment. Deployment of this tool (see Figure 13.9) led to immediate, substantial profit improvements. A disguised example illustrates the principles: instead of submitting an offer at a cost-plus-driven price of approximately €400,000 that sales managers would usually heavily discount, the company is now in a position to confidently offer its solution at €465,000. This price is low compared with the total quantified customer value of over €800,000. This process thus enables the company to sell its products with a robust ROI calculation attached. There is a price premium over low-cost competitors, and this is graciously acknowledged. The main

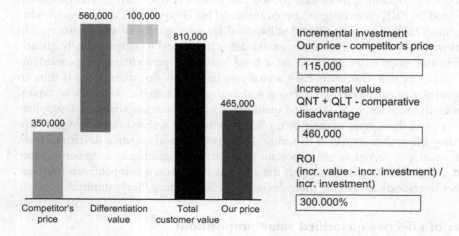

Figure 13.9 Quantifying the value proposition – a case study in B2B services.
(*Source*: Hinterhuber & Partners 2016)

point, however, is that an investment of approximately €100,000 (i.e., the price premium versus the low-cost competitor) leads to incremental customer benefits of over €400,000 (i.e., the difference in customer value between the two offers), thus leading to an ROI of 300 percent.

This is, in sum, a key benefit of value-based pricing and value quantification: turning the conversation from a discussion on price differences to an exploration and documentation of quantified customer benefits.

Value quantification is especially effective and in many cases mandatory when the supplier has a price premium over a relevant competitor. For many suppliers the key question is: Is it possible to convince customers that customers end up paying less by purchasing the most expensive offer? The quantified value proposition of SAP (Raihan 2010) provides an alternative way of presenting a premium-price offer: not as one that will lead to lower costs of ownership, but one that reduces customer risks (see Figure 13.10).

SAP sells enterprise software. In this specific project case, the company's price is 20 percent above the price of a comparable competitor. SAP argues that the true cost of the competitive solution is higher than its own price, mainly because risks have not been accounted for. SAP identifies several categories of risk: solution risk (lower business functionality, regulatory risk), supplier risk (only local presence, long-term viability), technology risk (lower scalability), operational risk (lower flexibility), and, finally, implementation risk (lower experience). These risks can be quantified and should be, at least according to SAP, added to the price of the lower-cost solution. The risk-adjusted price of the apparently low-cost offer exceeds the price of SAP's solution by a substantial amount. According to SAP's experience, this helps the company win deals even though the list price of its solution is substantially higher than the price of the customer's next best alternative. Lower risks thus can justify price premiums.

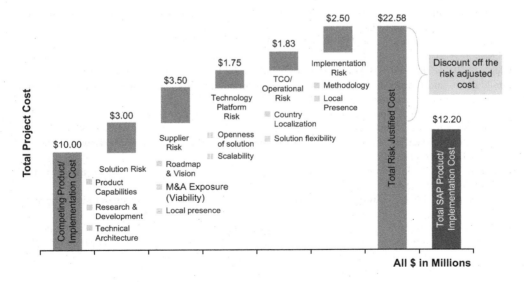

Figure 13.10 Quantifying the value proposition – the example of SAP.

Further considerations

Value quantification capabilities may be the most important capabilities of high-performing sales companies today. Building these capabilities requires a deep personal and organizational change. An interviewee at a global B2B IT service company observes: "What we started to realize was: It is not what your products or services do for your customers. It is what your customers are able to do as a result of using your products and services."

The preliminary results of this research indicate that companies with well-developed value quantification capabilities are able to realize higher prices and higher win rates. Relationships with customers benefit as well: collaboration increases. As companies implement the process outlined here – (1) customer insight, (2) value creation, (3) value proposition, (4) value quantification, and (5) implementation and documentation – customer satisfaction and loyalty typically increase. Thus, developing these capabilities may lead companies to achieve a sustainable competitive advantage.

We lack, however, quantitative empirical studies documenting the link between a company's value quantification capability and performance. This would make for a fascinating study.

Acknowledgments

This chapter is based on the article Hinterhuber, A., "Value quantification – the next challenge for B2B selling" in Hinterhuber, A., Liozu, S. (editors) *Pricing and the Sales Force*, Routledge, 2015. Copyright © 2016 Routledge. All rights reserved. Reprinted by permission.

References

Anderson, J., Kumar, N., and Narus, J. (2007) *Value Merchants: Demonstrating and Documenting Superior Value in Business Markets*, Boston, MA: Harvard Business School Press.

Anderson, J. C., Narus, J. A., and Van Rossum, W. (2006) "Customer value propositions in business markets," *Harvard Business Review* 84(3), 90–99.

Arnould, E. J. and Wallendorf, M. (1994) "Market-oriented ethnography: Interpretation building and marketing strategy formulation," *Journal of Marketing Research* 31(4), 484–504.

Cayla, J., Beers, R., and Arnould, E. (2014) "Stories that deliver business insights," *MIT Sloan Management Review* 55(2), 55–62.

Clegg, A. (2014, 21 October) "The quiet art of being a good listener," *Financial Times*, p. 12.

Drollinger, T. and Comer, L. B. (2013) "Salesperson's listening ability as an antecedent to relationship selling," *Journal of Business & Industrial Marketing* 28(1), 50–59.

Ernst & Young. (2002) "Fortune 1000 IT Buyer Survey: What could shorten sales cycles and further increase win rates for technology vendors?" Economics & Business Analytics white paper.

Gendron, G. and Burlingham, B. (1989) "The entrepreneur of the decade: An interview with Steven Jobs," *Inc* 10(4), 114–28.

Hinterhuber, A. (2004) "Towards value-based pricing – An integrative framework for decision making," *Industrial Marketing Management* 33(8), 765–78.

Hinterhuber, A. (2008) "Customer value-based pricing strategies: Why companies resist," *Journal of Business Strategy* 29(4), 41–50.

Hinterhuber, A. (2013) "Can competitive advantage be predicted? Towards a predictive definition of competitive advantage in the resource-based view of the firm," *Management Decision* 51(4), 795–812.

Hinterhuber, A. and Liozu, S. M. (2014) "Is innovation in pricing your next source of competitive advantage?" *Business Horizons* 57(3), 413–23.

Hinterhuber & Partners (2016) "Best practices in quantified value propositions." White paper, Innsbruck, Austria.
Hinterhuber, A. and Pollono, E. (2014) "Value-based pricing: The driver to increased short-term profits," *Finance & Management* 221(May), 21–24.
Hinterhuber, A. and Snelgrove, T. (2012) "Quantifying and documenting value in B2B," Professional Pricing Society online course, available at: www.pricingsociety.com/home/pricing-training/online-pricing-courses/quantifying-and-documenting-value-in-business-markets.
Lanning, M. J. and Michaels, E. G. (1988, July) "A business is a value delivery system," McKinsey & Company Staff Paper No. 41.
Liozu, S., Hinterhuber, A., Perelli, S., and Boland, R. (2012) "Mindful pricing: Transforming organizations through value-based pricing," *Journal of Strategic Marketing* 20(3), 1–13.
McMurchy, N. (2008) "Tough times in IT: How do you exploit the opportunities?" Gartner presentation. 1 December, Stamford, CT.
Meyrowitz, C. (2014) "The CEO of TJX on how to train first-class buyers," *Harvard Business Review* 92(5), 45–48.
Nagle, T. T. and Holden, R. K. (2002) *The Strategy and Tactics of Pricing: A Guide to Profitable Decision Making* (3rd ed.), Englewood Cliffs, NJ: Prentice Hall.
Raihan, R. (2010) "Leveraging IT to drive business value," presentation at the Information Resource Management Association of Canada (IRMAC), Toronto, Canada.
Rosenback, M. (2013) "Antecedents and obstacles to total cost of ownership analysis in industrial marketing – A case study," paper presented at the 29th IMP Conference, Atlanta, Georgia.
Snelgrove, T. (2013) "Creating Value That Customers Are Willing and Able to Pay For," presentation at the Product Management Forum of the Manufacturers Alliance for Productivity and Innovation (MAPI), Rosemont, IL.

14 Implementing pricing strategies via quantified value propositions

Todd Snelgrove

So your company has decided it wants to be the "value player" in your industry. Not only do you want to create customer value in the products, services, systems, and supporting services you bring, but you also want to get paid for that value. What are some of the key resources you need to create so that your sales and marketing teams are equipped, and that your value propositions resonate not only with the product or service user but also with the economic buyer? (think procurement). The ability to quantify in customer-centric measurements the value that your solution will provide versus the next best alternative – and, yes, an alternative always exists, including doing nothing – allows the customer, with the support of your compelling customized business case, to buy your "higher priced" offering. In addition to demonstrating how you can improve your customer's key performance indicators (KPIs), it's important to demonstrate how you can affect your customer's financials, such as return on investment (ROI), cash flow breakeven, and profit dollars saved or made, which will get executive management's attention.

Let me explain a little bit about my background and journey. As a non-technical person I ended up as product manager at SKF, an industrial engineering company, in the mid-1990s. At that time my boss made it clear that I should avoid purchasing – all they care about is price – and that all my work should be helping the sales and distributors reach the people who'd use our solutions, who'd benefit from them, and who'd have the budget to buy them. It was sound advice. In less than half a decade, though, I began noticing that we'd get a lot of interest from the technical buyer, the person who saw and understood the value of our solutions, but that procurement was either buying other, similar solutions, or saying no, or no budget money existed. A *black hole* existed, where all these great sales opportunities went to die a slow death. Research by the Corporate Executive Board shows that with the ever-expanding use of decision-by-committee, risk aversion, and rapidly changing business environments shifting customer priorities, it's no wonder (Toman, Adamson, and Gomez 2017).

Thus we began our first attempt at value quantification for one of the company's products: industrial bearings. We were preparing for a new product launch, we were focused on how and why the new solution would be better than the existing market offerings, and ours was only 20 percent more expensive. Our product featured more settings (flow rates) than our competitors' offerings. Note that all bearings need different types and amounts of grease based on the operating conditions. Our initial focus at product launch was that ours was more "accurate" (it could deliver the actual amount of grease that the bearing needed).

The competitors' devices could only be set to dispense a fixed amount of grease over 1, 3, 6, or 12 months, whereas ours could be set to dispense at any interval, regular or irregular. I learned that, in general (had to make an assumption), if I took 1,000 applications they are all so different – the amount of grease needed was divided equally over the 12 months. So what does this mean for the "more accurate unit" if the machine required the fixed amount of a unit's grease to be delivered over 1, 3, 6, 12 months? In general no incremental benefit existed using ours, as both systems could deliver that flow rate. However, what about when the machine needed that amount of grease over 2, 4, 5, 7, 8, 9, 10, 11 months? The other system couldn't deliver, so you were either over- or under-greasing – in both cases that's bad and a waste of money. So 8 out of 12 times the "older option" was wrong: 66 percent of the units being bought were not delivering the right amount of grease, assuming a conservative 33 percent reduction in units (the one you had set for 6 months really should be 10 months, or the one set at 1 month should have been at 2 months). Then the price "increase" created a lot of customer value based on reducing the number of units purchased. One industrial company went from 1,000 units a year at $25.00 ($25,000) to 585 units from SKF at $30.00 ($17,550), for an annual savings of over $7,450; in other words, a 20 percent price premium saved 30 percent of the total dollars they spent on these greasing systems. The units in use were now delivering the right amount of grease, which is what they were paying for (put another way, that's 415 units that they didn't need to install, dispose of, etc.).

It became clear with that order, and numerous subsequent ones, that we would not be able to get the customers to appreciate the difference unless we could convert that into dollars saved. So with what began on a piece of paper, then an Excel spreadsheet, then a neat-looking ROI tool, I began the creation of a program called Documented Solutions for SKF. When I left, it contained profiles of 174 solutions that could be documented using customer-specific information, along with over 105,000 cases approved by customers stating precisely the amount of value created for each customer, worth over $6 billion, that could be sorted by industry, customer, country, or other ways to allow sales to proactively build a business case, with so many references to support the assumptions.

In 2014 this program was recognized by the Strategic Account Management Association (SAMA) as 1 of the 50 best sales strategies over the last 50 years for the tool, process, and concept to help drive negotiating based on value.

Very quickly, the program evolved from one solution to many, for all industries that we covered. We then noticed that it was a demand and benefit in all regions of the world. With that, I became, to my knowledge, the first global vice president of value. Responsibilities included building value-based selling tools, helping the whole company get better at creating offerings that the customers really value, calculating that value, selling and communicating that value, and most importantly getting paid for that value. Figure 14.1 is a diagram that Professor James Anderson, the "Guru of Value" as I call him, and I created. The impetus, based on both our global work, was that other companies were following the lead and creating ROI/value-quantification tools, but that the results of these value initiatives were not translating into bottom-line benefits. Why? Research shows that too often customers only focus on helping sales and marketing with the *ability* to sell value, not on the ongoing *want* to sell value. I won't discuss each of these points in detail but will focus more on how value quantification allows value-based pricing (for a full review, see Hinterhuber and Snelgrove 2016). However, according to a 2017 SAMA survey, every company knew it needed to quantify customer value but only 30 percent did so, and my experience is that of those that did, all could be better at it (Snelgrove and Hinterhuber, 2017).

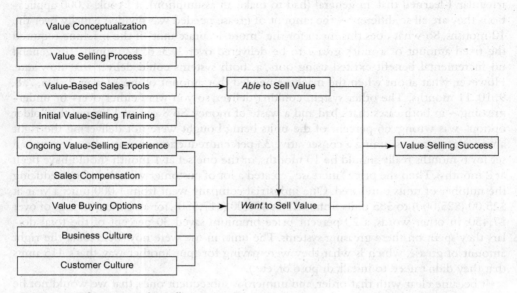

Figure 14.1 What causes value-selling success?
(*Source*: adapted from Snelgrove and Anderson 2016)

Value conceptualization

The following set of questions can help to guide sales, marketing, and strategic account managers in the process of developing the quantified value proposition.

In developing your new product/service, are you asking what this feature and benefit would be worth to a group of representative customers? Are you building the formulae and adding the test-case information of examples of the *improvement ranges* that customers are seeing versus the next best alternative, so that when a new offering is launched your tool includes a calculation with sample information for each segment that it's designed for?

Have you created a *value-selling process* that pushes sales and marketing to interact earlier in the buying cycle, where you are able to frame the discussion around value for the customer, versus reacting to existing demand in the request-for-quote phase and then trying to say "hey, but look at our value"?

Have you created a *tool for sales to create customized ROI analysis* for all solutions, one that is easy to use, makes sense for the customer, saves and tracks cases as you build them, and when customers adopt your solution you track the actual realized value?

Have you *trained your team to be able and comfortable to sell on value*? This does not mean one seminar and then everyone is an expert. It needs to be ongoing, robust, challenging, and thought provoking, with exercises, roleplaying, and tests along the way. Selling is a skill, and like any skill it needs regular training to improve.

Are *you rewarding the behavior you want* exhibited? Some companies measure sales versus targets. If so, why would I fight and push to get the customer to see that I shouldn't discount 5 percent and that my value is worth it, and maybe even enter into a hybrid value agreement? If the top line is all that's measured, it's easy for me to cut my sales by 5 percent and move along; however, 5 percent comes off the bottom line, and for most companies that's 50 percent of the net profit. One sign that you're not rewarding the right behavior is that sales employees spend more time pushing back on management, marketing, and pricing, and saying that they need a discount or that your company's prices are too high, which also means that you haven't equipped them with the right tools and knowledge to have the right conversation.

Have you created *contracts/agreements that allow the customer to pay based on the value actually received*? If not, how can the procurement experts believe that they will really get value buying your offering? If all you can offer are words or a few PowerPoint slides, you won't get the traction you want. Many companies have policies and processes for offering discounts, but what about ones that say "no discount, but I guarantee value delivery"? I discuss this in more detail later.

Business culture

What does your company stand for? Does your CEO talk about customer value, is it part of your annual report, do you discuss it at your investor day? For a business culture change to occur, this can't be a program run by someone as a one-off flavor of the month. Do you have a full-time person driving the concept, adoption, buy-in, and constant refreshment of your value differentiation strategy?

Customer culture

Are you engaging customers differently, at different and earlier times in the sales process to discuss and demonstrate that when they buy your product range that they should be buying on best value, not the lowest price that meets the minimum requirement set? Being seen as the subject-matter expert company in your industry, driving the change in how customers buy to be based on quantified value requires a different sales and marketing approach.

Value quantification

Before we delve more deeply into how to quantify, let's remind ourselves why we need to. When customers are choosing to buy anything, two things are occurring. They're thinking about their ability to pay (ATP) and their willingness to pay (WTP). Recall my discussion of what we saw happening with the black hole where opportunities went and nothing happened. ATP refers to whether the customer has the money to buy your offering, and WTP refers to whether they want to allocate a scarce resource (money) to your offering versus to some other needs. Quantifying your value using customer- or industry-specific numbers or averages addresses these two issues. With respect to the customer's ATP, certainly budgets are set and companies only have so much money; however, if you can make a believable business case demonstrating that your idea would save a million dollars a year, would pay for itself in 3 months, and for which you have 20 industry examples, the customer would find or reappropriate money from other needs to your solution. As a previous boss once said, "If I get a business case I believe, with low risk and high probability, I would borrow the money if I had to." Second is the customer's WTP. You're competing with other options for the customer's time and money; they have budgets set and your solution is not on the list. Another quote from my old boss: "I constantly reprioritize needs and capital allocation, based on the business case." So your new information technology offering is competing not only with others but also with the new factory that could be built in Asia to meet demand. In both scenarios, if you haven't done the work to quantify the value you'll deliver, how can you expect your customer to do your job for you?

There are a few important ways to use value quantification in the pricing process. First, when you're pricing a new offering, if you can quantify the expected range of benefit for the customer, versus other alternatives, then you'll know whether your solution is delivering more value than the competitor's offering, and if so, how much. You'll also know in certain industries, applications, and use scenarios how much value you'll be delivering, and you can set your price so that you receive "part" of that incremental benefit. What percentage of that benefit you should aim for would require a whole chapter itself. Look at it as a continuum: the greater the value (energy savings) and the quicker the payback, the more you can go for. I would pay 50 percent of the savings if it was happening in year 1, but if the savings accrue over a decade and the breakeven is in 3 years, I would be willing to pay less of the value (money) created.

Guaranteeing your value and getting paid based on that value is another important way to profit from quantifying it. In some cases – not the norm – if the customer is big enough, and if you can exercise enough control over the implementation of your offering, and data are available to measure the impact, you can enter into *performance-based agreements* (*PBAs*). You would need to agree on how value will be created and how to measure it so that your payment is solely based on actual performance. PBAs can be riskier but can also benefit both parties. You can also use them to support *value-based selling*, where you run the business case proactively and say to the customer that, "based on these assumptions and experiences, using your numbers you should get the following impact." This business case is used to "justify" your higher upfront price, but the implementation and the actual value received could be higher or lower depending on how the customer adopts and implements the offering. Finally, a *hybrid value agreement* has worked well for me. Demonstrating your company's ability to create and quantify value, and then saying "pay me my price (which is higher than the next best alternative) but I will guarantee X savings (10 percent)/profit improvement per year as a percentage of what you buy from me" assures the customer that you're along for the ride and that you're not just making a marketing/sales pitch. I spent much time explaining why an annual 10 percent improvement was better than a 10 percent price reduction, and most procurement people agreed, and this became a win-win scenario for both supplier and buyer. We won a coveted SAMA Supplier Excellence award in 2015 based on this model, for "impacting customer metrics using a joint scorecard." Again, we had to agree on what was of value (energy, water, increased production), the formulae for calculating it (the SKF Documented Solutions Program), and the numbers to use in the formulae (10 cents per KWh), as well as what SKF would earn if it met or exceeded the target and what it would have to do if it did not.

In the marketplace, where customers have stopped taking the time to evaluate your direct competitors, and where the differentiation you offer is perceived as increasingly diminishing, you must reframe all those value drivers that you deliver into the sole metric that all companies care about – money. As customers move more and more to committee buying decisions versus decisions made only by the end user, customizing your value for each stakeholder is mandatory, and all stakeholders care about what that value means for their bottom line. Also, when one stakeholder is being asked to pay for a benefit to another stakeholder (e.g., less unplanned downtime), the only metric that the economic buyer understands is the profit impact for their company. Interestingly, a Monitor Group (2011) study found that companies that have a strong execution on their "value based pricing strategy are 24% more profitable than others in their industry, and 36% more profitable than companies that have a strong execution on cost or share driven strategy." At the same time, procurement that buys based on an evolution from best value total cost of ownership (TCO) to total profit added is 35 percent more profitable (Manufacturers Alliance for Productivity and Innovation 2012). In other words, it's not a zero-sum game: buyers and sellers can both be more profitable. However, it's up to the sales, marketing, and pricing organization to do the work, quantify the value, demonstrate that value, and offer payment methods so that customers can pay for value realized. It's not easy, but it's possible, and the payback is huge, immediate, and a sustainable differentiator.

References

Hinterhuber, A. and Snelgrove, T. C. (eds) (2016) *Value First then Price: Quantifying Value in Business-to-Business Markets from the Perspective of Both Buyers and Sellers*, Routledge, New York.

Manufacturers Alliance for Productivity and Innovation (2012) *Approaches Towards Purchasing on Total Cost of Ownership*, A MAPI Council Survey, Arlington, VA.

Monitor Group (2011) Operating profit relative to industry peers [Figure 3], in *Pricing Capability Study*, www.monitor.com.

Snelgrove, T. C. and Anderson, J. (2016) "Muddling through on customer value in business markets?" in A. Hinterhuber and T. C Snelgrove (eds), *Value First then Price: Quantifying Value in Business-to-Business Markets from the Perspective of Both Buyers and Sellers*, Routledge, New York, pp. 28–38.

Snelgrove, T. and Hinterhuber, A. (2017) "Value First Then Price: Quantifying Value in Business to Business Markets from Both a Buyer and Sellers Perspective," Webinar, Strategic Account Management Association, Chicago, IL, 18 January, https://events.strategicaccounts.org/events/register.php?id=011817.

Toman, N., Adamson, B. and Gomez, C. (2017, March–April) "The new B2B sales imperative," *Harvard Business Review*, https://hbr.org/2017/03/the-new-sales-imperative.

15 Adopt value selling
Best practices to drive sustainable organizational change

Peyton Marshall

Value-based pricing provides tangible business results through better strategic decision-making (Liozu and Hinterhuber 2014). When pricing, product management, and marketing teams understand how their new products create value for their customers, they design more profitable offerings; focus on more appropriate customer segments; and set better, more realizable pricing strategies that reflect offer designs and customer segments. For products and solutions already on the market, teams that update their value-based pricing models regularly improve product performance over the product life cycle. Embedding value messages into marketing collateral makes marketing content more customer-centric. Teams monitoring value adapt faster and more proactively to changes in customer and competitor conditions.

The starting point for any value strategy initiative is a high-quality value model. Framing the model in terms of offerings, competitors, and customer segments is critical for clarity. The heart of a high-quality value model is a clear connection between differentiated features, differentiated benefits expressed as qualitative customer impacts, plausible and supportable quantitative advantages, and financial dollarized value drivers based on the economic value of an offering's differentiation. A good value model improves the quality of internal discussions by providing a better organizing framework for strategic product decisions.

Value selling: realize the potential value of differentiated offerings through better sales execution

Better decisions based on customer value are reason enough to transform an organization into a value-centric one, but the most substantial business impacts are only achieved through sales execution. Value selling improves sales results. Customer relationship management (CRM) data from business-to-business (B2B) organizations using value proposition software show that sales opportunities where a value proposition is used have 5 to 15 percent higher win rates and 5 to 25 percent higher price outcomes.

The success of value selling is a logical consequence of changes in technology and buying practices. Buyers, equipped with online information, need fewer live sales conversations to understand product features. Buyer organizations increasingly require documented rationale for purchases, including financial analysis and return on investment (ROI). Value selling moves sales teams beyond selling features to discussing how your solution delivers business outcomes to the buyer. A good value proposition articulates the qualitative results that your solution delivers, how it delivers them quantitatively and qualitatively, and what the impact is worth financially. Value selling is the natural and perhaps the only response to buyer empowerment.

The evidence is powerful that B2B organizations with differentiated products need to sell value, but changing commercial organizations is rarely straightforward. Even with strong value modeling skills and disciplines, and strong value modeling content, value-selling initiatives are not predestined for success. Before a review of best practices, consider the sources of failure.

Two reasons value-selling initiatives fail

The origin of a value-selling initiative often points to its most significant risk of failure. Value selling usually originates from one of two sources:

1. *Sales management* frequently realizes the need to sell on value. Deals lost on price and deals lost to no decision support this realization. Requests from the field for ROI analyses and business justifications highlight the need for skills and tools. The natural first response to this perceived need is sales skills training. Training programs are rarely relevant or impactful to sales unless (1) they are very specific to your solution, your competitive environment, and the circumstances relevant to your buyers; and (2) they provide simple and useful tools that support sales teams in buyer presentations and ongoing conversations about what your solution will deliver. Training sales reps who do math on a whiteboard or on the back of a napkin rarely result in a successful value-selling initiative. A few of the better sales representatives may learn from the sales course, develop their own approach and succeed, but their content is usually not accessible by others and their successful approaches are not deployed to other members of the team. There is an important ingredient in sales enablement that has to be deployed. Sales teams need solution-specific, sales-ready tools and content that help them discuss and quantify value quickly to support scalable value selling. High-quality value models need to be generated and transformed into value propositions that are simple, usable, tested sales tools.
2. *Product management and marketing professionals* often decide that sales teams need value-selling tools. This is a natural extension of their responsibility to provide creative, high-quality content for use in sales. The quantification content, often in the form of a value calculator, is usually created by product managers who tend to understand how your solution works and how your customers benefit from your solution. The visual formatting and refinement of the content may benefit from involvement by marketing professionals skilled in design and messaging. The resulting output often reflects the deep knowledge of the product manager, but just as often fails to reflect the sales process. The predictable result is an overcomplicated calculator, launched by a product manager at a national sales meeting to inattentive sales reps who never use it. There will be no adoption of value selling if the value content has not been (1) tested by sales users in customer situations, and (2) refined and simplified by marketing based on sales feedback. There will be no adoption by sales users of value tools if their own sales management does not strongly sponsor the value-selling program, push the early adoption of value selling through their regular meetings, and publicize value-selling success stories.

Value-selling successes and failures both provide strong organizational pointers on some fundamentals of an organization's culture required to drive success. Both sales and product management/marketing teams need to be accountable and need to be aligned.

Sales and marketing alignment: value propositions to fit the sales process

For value selling to succeed, value propositions need to be designed to fit an organization's sales approach and sales methodology. While there are many variations in sales approaches, a simple roadmap based on a *buyer's* process can be used to understand how value propositions support sales-team objectives in light of buying objectives. Buying processes may differ by business and by the purchases under consideration, but most B2B organizations operate sequentially as they work through a decision to change and a decision to buy. First, buyers identify and prioritize new alternatives before selecting alternatives for evaluation (usually by committee) before they engage in the contractual, negotiation, and approval processes that it takes to make a financial commitment (see Figure 15.1).

Early in a buying process, sales aims to connect with potential buyer sponsors, qualifying individuals and accounts while differentiating your solution. The goal is to get sponsors, who are willing and able to commit time and resources, to evaluate your solution. The objective at this early stage is not to prove that you are better but to move the buyer forward. This stage is usually navigated by a sales rep with limited support from presales members of the broader sales team. This stage does not require a lot of customization, math, or proof. A Forrester survey (Lindwall 2017) shows that the likelihood of eventual sales-team success increases threefold if sales reps can establish themselves early as the first vendor to communicate a clear vision of value. Presenting customer value early in the form of a flexible case study is natural early in the sales cycle. Using value early increases qualified sales opportunities and moves buyers forward to invest their time and energy in evaluation (see Figure 15.2).

In the *middle* of the process, additional sales-team members often get involved as buyer teams evaluate your solution. In broadening the team-to-team dialogue, it's important that your sales-team members establish their credentials and engage customer stakeholders to

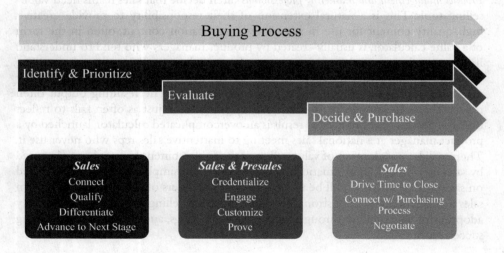

Figure 15.1 The buying process.
(*Source*: image courtesy of LeveragePoint Innovations, Inc. 2017)

Figure 15.2 Value propositions support continuous value communication.
(*Source*: image courtesy of LeveragePoint Innovations, Inc. 2017)

position themselves as trusted advisers. At this point, customizing a solution is often a key objective. Being ready to prove, or at least persuade, stakeholders that your solution is better for that buyer is usually necessary. A strong value proposition can make the transition in the middle of the sales cycle from being a flexible case study into being a more tailored, more specific customer-value analysis.

Later in the buying process, sales teams use value propositions to achieve their primary objectives in closing the right deal at the right price. At this stage, there is a need for speed and a need to stay connected to the purchasing process. Value propositions drive speed in a buying process when a buying sponsor understands the deliverable in terms of a business case to buy shared with a sales account executive. That shared business case becomes a stronger basis for sales to remain engaged in an otherwise opaque and inaccessible procurement process. Perhaps most important, a great value proposition becomes a strong basis for negotiating price–value trade-offs confidently, based on the deeper customer understanding created by a value proposition.

How to accelerate a value-selling initiative

Broad value-selling rollouts are eventually appropriate, but piloting value selling to get early successes is usually the right approach. The initial benefits and successes that result from the pilot generate early momentum. Internal promotion then spreads the word among sales professionals and sales management. One success becomes a trend. A results-driven sales culture and incentives will take over from there to make value selling viral.

There are four key ingredients for a successful value-selling pilot:

1. *A strong value proposition.* A value proposition is different from, and better than, a value calculator. Sales professionals get lost in most value calculators because they over-emphasize assumptions and math. In contrast, value propositions help to tell a story. They highlight simple messages. What do you do for your customer? What customer problems or challenges can your solution address? What are the two or three ways you deliver customer value? How are you different? Strong value propositions provide options to discuss quantitative and financial benefits, but first they highlight customer problems and the qualitative ways that your solution can address those problems. They do not force sales users to go too deep, too fast in customer conversations. As content, value propositions are often most impactful when they pivot on a relevant customer case study that has the flexibility to be adapted to other buyers. For a pilot to succeed, the value proposition needs to focus on a good target offering. Differentiated, strategically important, and high ROI offerings are the right focus for initial value propositions. To assess whether an offering is a good candidate for piloting, consider

its value proposition score. The (number of reps) times (average sales value) times (closes per year) equals a score that shows the revenues that value selling can impact. The outcome metrics to measure value-selling success and the benefits of value selling are simple math on those target revenues: 5 to 15 percent of those revenues from higher closing rates, 5 to 25 percent of those revenues from higher prices. Increases of that magnitude should be worth the time and attention of sales leaders and sales professionals (see Figures 15.3 and 15.4).

2. *Engage a sales leader.* Product managers and marketing professionals sometimes think they can roll out great content to sales themselves. Product manager presentations are never enough. Sales change requires sponsorship by sales management. There are too many organizational imperatives in most B2B organizations that compete for sales professionals' time and bandwidth. Sales leaders need to sponsor value selling as an important priority because employees generally listen to ideas from their bosses more closely than they listen to ideas that are good on their own merits. Good ideas coming from management are the most persuasive ideas of all. Sales leadership is critical to a successful rollout effort. Ideally, sales leadership should participate in choosing the right offer to target. Feedback from the sales leader on value proposition content should be sought and incorporated. The sales leader should choose and motivate the right sales people for an initial push, including the sales mobilizer. The sales leader should participate in and drive a results webinar.

3. *Engage, motivate, and support a sales mobilizer.* A sales mobilizer is key to the success of an initial value-selling push. A sales mobilizer is someone who presents to customers on at least a semi-regular basis. The sales mobilizer should ultimately be responsible

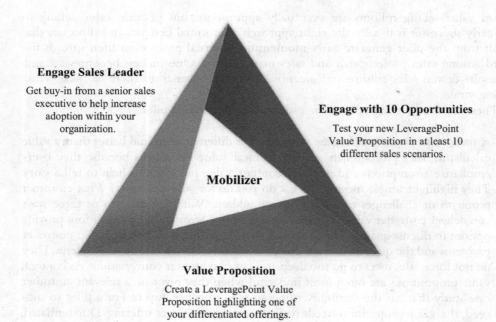

Figure 15.3 Key ingredients for success.

(*Source*: image courtesy of LeveragePoint Innovations, Inc. 2017)

Adopt value selling 147

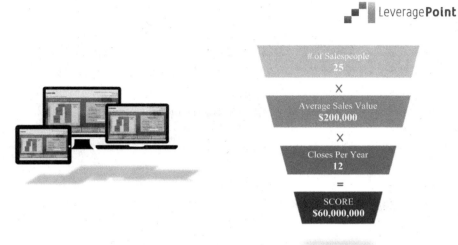

Figure 15.4 Value proposition score: target offering.
(*Source*: image courtesy of LeveragePoint Innovations, Inc. 2017)

for the execution of the value-selling pilot, and that accountability should be clearly communicated by the sales leader. As a result, the sales mobilizer is the right person to test the value proposition and provide early feedback to product management and marketing for refinement. A good sales mobilizer gets comfortable with the value proposition, uses it in one or more customer conversations, then records a video, available to other reps involved, showing *how* they would present the value proposition to a customer. This provides useful context and ideas for other reps in their call preparation as they get ready for a value conversation. A good sales mobilizer is a team player who is ready to present with other sales-team members and to assist other sales people in their preparation to use the value proposition. The sales mobilizer should report directly to the sales leader on the value-selling initiative and should be empowered to enlist the sales leader in changing sales behavior.

4. *Engage with at least ten opportunities*. Success in sales requires the courage to try, fail, learn, and try again. One and done is never a true test of value selling. Testing a value proposition in at least ten sales scenarios should provide enough experience to work out the kinks, learn what works, and see how it works. The early payoffs are not necessarily hard dollar payouts: a good meeting, a target who begins to talk about their business and can't stop, a compliment from a target customer, and/or learning enough about account specifics from a value conversation to stop wasting time on the opportunity. Closed deals follow these initial benefits downstream in the sales cycle, providing key success metrics to evaluate the initiative and to motivate sales in a broader rollout. The process of tracking results from ten sales scenarios provides discipline and structure for a sales mobilizer, helping to push others to obtain more shots on goal, following up on value conversations, and capturing customer feedback (see Figure 15.5).

Value Proposition Score	$60,000,000		Sales Leader	Charlotte Kinski
Results Target Date	end of Q3 2018		Sales Mobilizer	Rick Boggs

Opportunity	Opportunity Size	Sales Rep	Outcome
Value Precision Instruments	$350k	Rick Boggs	Deal closed–no price negotiation
Petty Transmissions Asia	$200k	Toni Perry	Customer kept challenging relevance of our benefits to their business. Stopped pursuing.
Cleveland Tool	$250k	Kate MacMurray	Good early meeting. Agreed to PoC. Deal now in procurement
Chronometrica	$150k	Bob Wolfowitz	Initial contact agreed to introduce others to value meeting.
Tangerine Software	$450k	Jerome Pearce	Initial skepticism about our benefits but agreed to follow-up meeting with product manager.

Figure 15.5 Value proposition experience: track results.

(*Source*: image courtesy of LeveragePoint Innovations, Inc. 2017)

Map for value-selling success: a checklist

There is a process that works in getting value selling underway. Following is a simple checklist that is effective in driving initial sales adoption of value selling at a time before there is evidence of success (see Figure 15.6).

- *Sales-ready value proposition.* Pick an important, differentiated product with a high score. Make sure the value proposition helps a rep tell a story. Focus messages on the customer while including quantitative and financial value statements. Be prepared to test and refine the value proposition based on direct feedback from sales professionals using it.

Status	Milestone	Results
✔	Value Proposition	Strong Value Proposition with score of $60 mm
✔	Engage Sales Leader	Presented Value Prop to Charlotte Kinski –5/1/18
✔	Mobilizer	Rick Boggs nominated by Kinski –5/3/18
✔	Video Complete?	Completed 6/28/18
✔	Engage with 10 Opportunities	Have closed one deal in the first five opportunities. Further opportunities identified
–	Success webinar complete?	Targeting end of August

Figure 15.6 Success map: target offering.

(*Source*: image courtesy of LeveragePoint Innovations, Inc. 2017)

- *Engage the sales leader.* Great content and hard work deserve sponsorship. Sales leaders can obtain the focus that gets the results. Enlist a strong sales leader to pick team members, kick off calls, provide general guidance, and ensure sales receptivity and disciplined follow-up.
- *Identify and support a sales mobilizer.* Sales mobilizers should have a stake in the value proposition's success and should be incentivized to support their team members. A credible, motivated sales mobilizer drives testing and use of the value proposition by designated sales-team members, providing experience in presenting the value proposition and experience in using it in customer conversations.
- *Record a presentation video.* Recording a short video of how the sales mobilizer would present the value proposition provides a test in its own right. The act of preparing for the video, recording it, and watching it improves the sales mobilizer's confidence in an initial presentation. The quality of the recording improves as a result. The wider impact is that other salespeople watch the presentation video, as it suits them, as part of their own preparation for initial use. The presentation video provides continuing, self-paced sales training that is often more valuable than a mandatory conference call.
- *Engage with ten opportunities.* Active encouragement and success stories overcome the fear of trying a new approach. Monitoring activity provides a second and strong incentive for sales-team members to innovate. Energetic follow-up by the sales mobilizer to make sure that members are identifying opportunities is important. Conference calls to compare results, with the sales leader on the call, generate momentum in realizing and documenting success.
- *Complete the initial phase with a success webinar.* The successes of an initial small sales team are an achievement that needs to be broadcast. Waiting for the next annual sales meeting to publicize how value selling worked and the value delivered is usually too long a wait. Complete the initial push. Consolidate the results and the successes. Then get the sales leader and the sales mobilizer in a required success webinar to drive adoption more widely. Follow-on internal campaigns celebrating success are important, but the success webinar should be the main event to kick off and drive broader sales rollout and adoption. Broader adoption becomes the key for measured outcomes and realized value metrics.

Value propositions for customer-centric selling

Value-selling programs focus sales teams on what you do for your customers. For account executives, value propositions are useful early in the sales cycle as flexible case studies in call preparation, in building sales confidence, in qualifying opportunities, and in engaging customer executives. For technical sales and presales professionals, joining the team in the middle of the sales process, value propositions provide customer-value analyses as an important consultative selling tool that directly address presales challenges. As customers decide to purchase, the value proposition becomes a shared business case, collaboratively agreed-upon between sales executives and customer sponsors, that serves as a buyer's internal financial justification to purchase and a sales team's asset in a price negotiation.

Great commercial organizations compete with their competitors and partner with their customers. Executing on this organizational vision extends pricing, product management, and marketing beyond internal analysis. Creating sales-ready value propositions aligns marketing with sales teams and with customers by delivering the best foundation for customer conversations. Value propositions provide core sales content that helps sales teams collaborate with buyers, communicating what your solution does for them. Implementing value propositions successfully in sales converts the value of differentiation into realized profitability.

References

Lindwall, M. (2017, July 10) "To win against increasing competition, equip your salespeople with a deeper understanding of your buyers," retrieved from https://go.forrester.com/blogs/14-01-27-to_win_against_increasing_competition_equip_your_salespeople_with_a_deeper_understanding_of_your_buy/.

Liozu, S.M. and Hinterhuber, A. eds (2014) *The ROI of Pricing: Measuring the Impact and Making the Business Case*, London: Routledge.

16 Executing price control in five simple steps

Mitchell D. Lee

Introduction

The fundamental ideas that drive the process of maximizing every margin moment are simple:

- a business should be selling its products and services at the highest price that each customer is willing to pay, and
- it should be paying as little as it can for the costs incurred to produce and deliver those products and services.

Squeezing the most out of that space between price and cost is all about attending to many, many details within a business. In an attempt to drive growth, most companies pick apart cost. While those strategies are of course helpful, the profit lever with the greatest impact is price (see Figure 16.1). Using this lever and executing to set the right price is done in light of several complex issues, however.

Complex, global enterprises must account for many business units and regions; countless customers and customer segments; many product lines; and hundreds, thousands, even hundreds of thousands of SKUs. It's a juggling act that requires balancing a mind-boggling number of variables to achieve the kind of commercial excellence that leads to truly maximized margins.

With so many moving parts to get into motion at the outset, the process of just starting out can be daunting for organizations seeking greater profitability. Nevertheless, it's important to remember that every journey begins somewhere. The key is to concentrate on a few key areas at first to build early momentum and then drive incremental improvement from there.

You certainly have dedicated resources focused on costs – your procurement function watches everything you buy and is probably getting more done for your company by becoming more centralized. The group is charged with controlling your costs.

But how do your dedicated pricing resources measure up? Do you have a group charged with controlling prices? Are you leveraging best practices with clear key performance indicators (KPIs) to show how your strategy is being executed in all your markets? Taking control of pricing by consolidating information, formalizing policies, and standardizing language and practices should be your first step toward systematically increasing your organization's growth and profitability.

"Systematically" is the key word here.

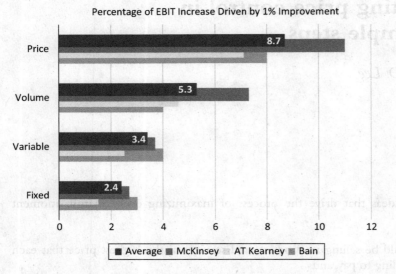

Figure 16.1 Price is your biggest price lever. Research shows that of the three key profit levers – price, volume, and cost – it's price that can make the largest bottom-line impact for any organization.

Some margin-focused organizations that recognize the need to charge more and raise the floor on pricing will try to roll it out simply by decree. But without the means to systematically control prices, what most customers end up paying doesn't universally reflect the decree. Without appropriate controls and pricing guidance, salespeople find new exceptions to drive prices down for each customer and each product in all their new deals.

Often that pricing guidance and control also needs to be paired with measurement to factually know what is going on within a sales environment so that decisions are informed by data rather than gut feel.

Too often, organizations find it hard to even have granular visibility into their executed pricing adjustments to recognize that a mandate for pricing change isn't being enforced. Simply proving out the failure requires inordinate amounts of work to gather spreadsheets and relevant information and manually crunch the data. By the time that work is complete, attention has shifted to the next big deal, and there's no time available to incorporate learnings.

This is why a systematic methodology backed by sound automation should be the first order of business in maximizing margins. And why measurement capabilities for feedback into your control process are critical.

Five steps to controlling price

Step 1: Consolidate pricing-related information into a single system

You can't control something unless you measure it. Organizations frequently struggle to gain visibility into less-than-profitable deals because pricing-related information is scattered across the enterprise.

It's crucial to remember that when gathering pricing-related information, transaction data are just one part of the relevant data. Transaction data are important, but it's very likely that there are other factors influencing pricing decisions.

Many executives recognize the commonsense need to gather pricing information into a single system so that it can act as a single source of truth for those making pricing decisions. It's obvious that doing so can reduce the number of conflicts and different versions of pricing schemes from creeping across business units, different sales teams, and so on. However, what's often overlooked is that this singular information pool isn't effective if it's limited to historical, transactional information.

Pricing-related information includes a lot of other information that may be collected internally and that may also occur externally but might never be tracked. Examples of this kind of data include

- customer attributes,
- seasonal information,
- regional data, and
- maybe even weather patterns – for example, ice cream sells on the first hot day, but not so much on the second and third hot days.

So, it's crucial not only to begin pooling pricing data into a single consolidated system but also to expand what you might traditionally define as pricing information when you begin the consolidation.

Organizations essentially need to cast a wide net and bring it all into a singular data lake. And if they want to ensure that they don't miss crucially relevant data points, they will need a solution that can automatically assess the important data and make suggestions for inclusion and consideration.

Step 2: Organize price information by a precise flow of influencing factors that contribute to ultimate price decisions

Consolidated price-related information in a single system will provide the business an important and authoritative body of data to which they can refer. But its true power will come from how all the data are organized and ultimately used.

To effectively control pricing, businesses should consider organizing pricing data around the idea of a waterfall. There is a cascade of influences in how a standard list price or generic starting price is successively adjusted or discounted to get down to not only the customer's negotiated price but also the net or pocket price. It's crucial to define the various steps along that waterfall that influence ultimate price points, including decisions, approval processes, and other variables.

Key concept: Use a price waterfall

You need agreement and understanding within your organization for pricing terms, so that everyone is on the same page. The price waterfall (see Figure 16.2) is an essential tool for organizing and visualizing all the commercial decisions that impact pricing and profitability across all business dimensions. With these definitions, accountability and responsibility for each action are clear.

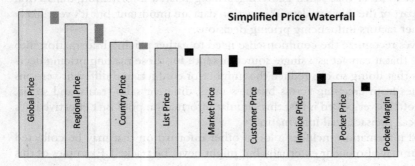

Figure 16.2 Simplified price waterfall. The price points shown in the gray bars depend on the commercial decisions collected in the black adjustment bars. Not all organizations will have each of these price points, and most will have a few adjustments bars between critical price points for greater granularity.

It may seem trivial, but getting agreement across the organization for these terms or others that your company uses in a similar manner is critical.

The price adjustments made between each of these price points is where the real accountability and execution are controlled. There may be only one person responsible for determining the adjustment between global price and regional price (within a central pricing group, for example). There are often several types of adjustments made by several groups between invoice price and pocket price, however. Determining the necessary granularity for your waterfall must strike a balance between ease of categorization (putting several types of adjustments into a single category) and loss of specificity (making it more difficult to determine root causes and accountability).

The factors of this pricing waterfall should be put in organizationally appropriate terms that track back to the business and business-unit policies – who had the decision-making responsibility for execution – and how execution is tracking against your strategy and tactics.

So, for example, you may begin first with a very general starting price or a standardized list price. From there you could have a regionally adjusted list price, and then the customer-category price. That leads to a jump-off point from which you might begin negotiating with the customer.

As you begin organizing pricing information into the waterfall, you may find that your business has four or five "touches" to a price before negotiations even start. Understanding not only the definitions of those touches but also the approval processes that trigger them will be the start to instituting price controls.

If an organization can see how the flow works, they can begin to understand the points throughout the waterfall where price changes must be instituted before sales even has their first interactions with customers to discuss the starting point for negotiation.

Ultimately, organizing in the waterfall format should help the organization understand and explain what a price means and by which process a specific price for a specific customer was developed. The business should have documented visibility into who approved an adjustment and why the decision was made. This is key for understanding the profitability of not only specific customer and product intersections, but also general pricing strategies around product families or customer segments.

That visibility should also include views into approval processes, which explain who made a particular decision, who has the approval levels to make certain exceptions, where they need to get permissions from to make changes, and how frequently changes are made. Ideally it should also provide the business reason for seeking approval for the exception. Getting visibility into approvals can help the business ask important questions that will drive more margin-friendly decisions:

- Was that approval reason justified?
- Would you do it again, in a similar situation?
- Should that result be encouraged or prevented in the future?

Step 3: Establish a common lexicon and organizational framework for discussing pricing decisions across the enterprise

Enterprises will inevitably be running distributed teams across various business units and regions that may have different pricing policies and objectives. As organizations roll out various price-control and margin-optimization pilot projects, it's important to set a level playing field so that even if certain teams follow variations of your rules and processes, they're at least speaking the same language when they discuss how pricing decisions are made.

Doing so enables fact-based comparisons within and between business units. When definitions are uniform across the organization, conversations become more meaningful as executives begin rolling up the numbers. Otherwise you get one business group saying list price when they mean regional price, another saying market price when they mean end-use, another saying sector price when they mean a specific geography. It gets even more uncertain and fuzzy when the conversation turns to profit margin: What's involved in the assumptions around the costs that are used? What's in, out, averaged, lagged, fully loaded?

Pricing control is a precise exercise, and that begins with precise language.

It's crucial that the terminology and the overall framework be universal, so that when someone in India talks about profit margins, someone in South America knows exactly what steps their Asian colleagues took to get there. Not only that: this common lexicon makes it easier for different teams to more quickly learn from one another, and momentum in one part of the business can more easily be transferred elsewhere.

Finally, with the agreed-upon definitions and waterfall structure, pricing KPIs may be constructed for easy and meaningful communication of pricing performance. For example, comparing a pocket price as a percentage of market price across sales organizations could surface high-performing or low-performing situations requiring further attention.

Step 4: Use artificial intelligence (AI) and automation to quickly identify opportunities and risks in customer behavior

Once an organization begins to thoroughly consolidate their pricing-related information and categorize it, they'll find that consolidating and categorizing all that information, formerly scattered across the enterprise, is just step 1 in gaining better control over pricing.

To really get the most value out of all that data, organizations need a way to quickly analyze it and to make swift decisions based on that information. However, with so many geographies, so many customers, so many product lines, so many SKUs, and so much data about the entire ecosystem, it's nearly impossible for human analysis to efficiently crunch it all and turn it into prescriptive advice for maximizing each margin moment.

This is where good analytics algorithms, AI, and automation come into play. AI identifies business behavior problems and solutions that even the best in-house data scientists can't manually spot in time to make effective business decisions. This is where AI-driven segmentation based on willingness to pay and pricing guidance based on business attributes for each of those segments really delivers.

If you think about the continuum of pricing guidance (see Figure 16.3), analytics can help process transactional data – and even forward-looking information – to deliver context and insights no matter where your organization is along the spectrum:

- Stage 0 is ad hoc, and largely gut-driven by sales in the field.
- Stage 1 begins to incorporate costs to understand margin impact but is very much internally focused.
- Stage 2 applies basic segmentation on the basis of customer groups and/or product groups but lacks the ability to differentiate at the intersection of product and customer, relying instead on simple floor pricing across large groups.
- Stage 3 shows initial signs of intelligent guidelines through the use of AI to operationalize pricing processes, yielding formal pricing envelopes (list, target, floors for approval levels).
- Stage 4 fully uses AI and robust, data-driven process operationalization to generate many (100-plus) customer/product segments based on willingness to pay, with specific pricing guidance generated for each segment.

In a price-control scenario, this means that with the right system solution, AI can automatically adjust price guidance and decisions based on current data from previous transactions –

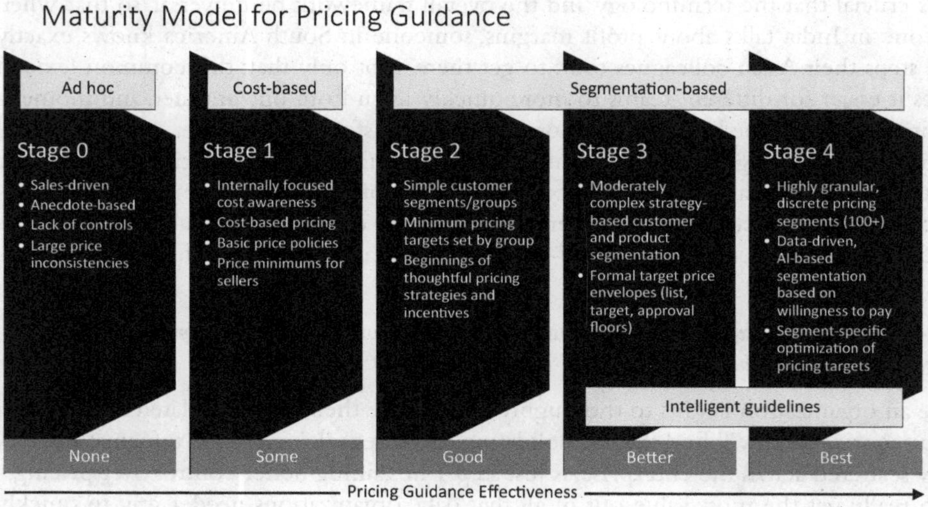

Maturity Model for Pricing Guidance

Ad hoc	Cost-based	Segmentation-based		
Stage 0	**Stage 1**	**Stage 2**	**Stage 3**	**Stage 4**
• Sales-driven • Anecdote-based • Lack of controls • Large price inconsistencies	• Internally focused cost awareness • Cost-based pricing • Basic price policies • Price minimums for sellers	• Simple customer segments/groups • Minimum pricing targets set by group • Beginnings of thoughtful pricing strategies and incentives	• Moderately complex strategy-based customer and product segmentation • Formal target price envelopes (list, target, approval floors)	• Highly granular, discrete pricing segments (100+) • Data-driven, AI-based segmentation based on willingness to pay • Segment-specific optimization of pricing targets
			Intelligent guidelines	
None	Some	Good	Better	Best

Pricing Guidance Effectiveness →

Figure 16.3 Pricing guidance maturity model. Maturity in pricing guidance can also depend on the specific products and services being offered. In every case, it's important to understand your position relative to your competition and the benefits in moving to more mature methodologies.

and bring your assessment of future conditions into play for consideration of next steps. Organizations should seek out automation that can get them as far along this continuum as possible.

Step 5: Take advantage of best practices already established by industry peers

While pricing strategies will always differ by industry and business, it's important to recognize that any organization can benefit from best practices established by industry peers. Many leaders see how many moving parts there are to implementing price optimization, and complexity scares them off. It's daunting, they don't know where to begin, and inaction often results.

The point is that not only do you not have to do everything at once, you also don't have to start from scratch.

There are already many best practices established. This includes information both about setting strategy and tactically executing on that strategy. Ideally, an organization should be working from industry-standard playbooks that provide guidance on tactical execution measures in controlling price. A playbook can help organize the review of the data and things to look for, to take action and improve what you're seeing. The very best playbooks help organizations continuously improve with the closed-loop cycle in making pricing decisions: decision, execution, measurement, and feedback.

Begin by taking measurements and connecting those measurements to what the business says it wants to do with pricing strategy. Evaluate how well you're executing against those strategies by using the playbook. The playbook will not only help you step through the process, it will also help you measure your progress along the way – KPIs that are oriented to that specific tactical execution.

How pricing systems can help

Price control is step 1 in achieving the kind of commercial excellence that leads to consistent maximization of margin. Begin by analyzing your data, discovering what's currently going on, and then make price strategy improvement policies. Then it is a matter of having both a methodology and the automation to consistently execute on those policies. Purpose-built pricing systems will help you drive the high-level pricing objectives down into the business for efficient execution.

- Having a consolidated data lake of pricing information generates the context, insight, and intelligence necessary to recommend relevant pricing targets and guidance.
- Deploying a consistent, referenceable, and repeatable analysis framework will help businesses streamline and organize decision data.
- A business-wide framework and common lexicon for control and measurement will ensure that everyone is on the same page for all pricing principles, decisions, and strategies.
- Advanced analytics algorithms and AI within pricing systems provide decision support and automation around price policies.
- Pricing-system vendors hold a wide body of knowledge about industry best practices. Leverage that broad experience as you establish your specific playbooks.

Dedicated, purpose-built, and enterprise-capable pricing systems help ensure that your business processes are consistently applied. With business-system integration (with systems such as enterprise resource planning [ERP] and customer relationship management [CRM] solutions), the execution of your strategies can be measured for effectiveness.

Implications for pricing execution

Many businesses previously changed prices infrequently, perhaps only once a year, because managing the mechanics was too hard: too many disconnected, standalone systems, and too many manually generated spreadsheets bridging the gaps. Following the five steps outlined here will yield effective and dynamic price control. You can have a simplified, well-understood process for operationalizing your pricing execution in business conditions that were previously too complex to rapidly reflect market conditions.

With your business strategies and tactics incorporated into your pricing execution, your prices can always be specific: the right price, for the right product, to the right customer, at the right time. This granularity lets you make decisions that maximize margin in each business opportunity.

Having agreed-upon measurements and well-understood processes ensures disciplined execution of your business-pricing process and yields two key organizational benefits, reflected in the Pareto principle, or the 80/20 rule. First, 80 percent of your decisions are now aligned with your goals and can flow through your process for execution with little or no intervention – everyone in the commercial process sees the measurements and understands how to make the process work faster and greatly increase business and sales velocity. Second, the resulting time savings is now available for careful consideration of the 20 percent of your decisions that really drive strategic results for your business.

Finally, it's important to base your price execution and control in an integrated, enterprise-level system, where the performance can be measured for feedback into control adjustments: find what practices are working well, and replicate; find what's failing, and eliminate.

17 Eight best practices to improve pricing execution

Stephan M. Liozu

Nothing happens in pricing without strong execution plans: it's a given. At the same time, many organizations struggle with their execution discipline. Projects lag behind, adoption rates are not as expected, and the payback expectations are not achieved. A pricing strategy might look good on paper but is worthless until it's implemented and embedded in the fabric of the organization.

A strong culture and discipline of execution do not come out of anywhere. They also don't appear overnight. Business and pricing leaders need to design their pricing strategies and programs with execution in mind. They must also candidly evaluate the level of execution discipline in the organization and integrate that into their project planning. Recognizing execution weaknesses or gaps early in the design of pricing programs is the best way to pay attention to execution early in the design process.

This chapter proposes eight best practices to boost a culture that might lead to superior pricing project execution. Some of these might fall under the pricing team's influence or control. Others might not be feasible. They are listed in no particular order.

1. Define the right key performance indicators (KPIs) to focus on execution

Defining success early in the design process of a pricing project is essential. When do we know if we've succeeded? This determination is easy for some of the traditional quantitative pricing KPIs. It's less obvious for the cultural and change management KPIs. The project team needs to focus on the most critical pricing and change KPIs and get consensus from the project team that these are the right ones. Buy-in from all relevant functions is essential: sales, marketing, pricing, finance, and top management. Two types of KPIs are usually recommended:

- Financial and pricing indicators: gross margin ($ or %), earnings before interest and taxes (EBIT) margin, average sales pricing ($), year-on-year price erosion, price realization versus budget, and many more. These are the financial KPIs driving the execution of the specific pricing project.
- Change management indicators: these typically focus on adoption, assimilation, and proficiency of a new tool, system, approach, discount structure, or whatever it is that we are deploying. The goal is to be able to gauge whether change is happening and to see whether people are learning and assimilating. Examples are the percentage of the population that has been trained, average minutes per pricing transaction in a new system, number of invoicing errors or credit notes issued due to pricing error, and average time spent in a new app.

The logical next question is how many KPIs are necessary to measure execution planning and reporting. There's no magic number, but a good rule of thumb is 8 to 12. It will depend on your ability to quickly collect the data and extract the numbers. Another consideration is the possible automation of the KPI calculation that needs to be reviewed during the project steering committee meeting or during the pricing council meetings.

2. Use dashboards to promote execution

Once the KPIs are agreed upon, the next step is to prepare a pricing dashboard or cockpit. The dashboard related to a specific project can be used as a powerful reminder of the project and as a promoter of pricing execution. There are considerations of design, data visualization, frequency of publication, selection of the population that needs to receive it, and confidentiality. A good dashboard is visually attractive and easy to read, and should focus on exceptions and corrective actions. Bad dashboards are boring, crowded, illogical, or too theoretical.

3. Mobilize your project management office (PMO)

Many organizations have PMOs at the corporate level to assist in large-scale project deployment. Having access to a PMO can make a difference in the execution of a pricing project, especially for large-scale projects or multi-year transformations. PMOs can assist with templates, systems, dashboards, resource planning, and consulting. If you get lucky, project managers can be assigned to support your project for free or for an internal fee. If you're even luckier, the PMO will have done work on previous pricing initiatives and might be able to dig up lessons learned, old documents, and other nuggets that might save you some time. More likely, a PMO might help you in the design of the project and let you manage execution on your own. It doesn't hurt to ask, though.

4. Learn about change management

Similarly, your organization might have professional change managers on staff. That's a blessing, especially if they have proper certification and recognized skills. Remember that project management and change management are not the same thing. Project management focuses on the technical side of change, while change management addresses the people side of change. Some PMOs train their staff in both disciplines. If your organization does not have a PMO and a change management function, you might have to learn about both on your own as you are designing your pricing strategies and/or pricing projects. There are digital courses and professional certifications available. Some of your team members might be certified project management professionals (PMPs). So make sure to seek knowledge and bring project and change management into your execution planning.

5. Bring value or pricing coaches to your team

When you feel you're on your own and need some reinforcement, ask the human resources team or organization development whether the organization has access to specialized coaches to support challenging projects. Remember that not all coaches are created equal. Some focus more on individual personal development while others specialize in high-performance team development. There are specialized value and pricing coaches available for hire. A good pricing coach should have both deep technical understanding and change management experience. Review the credentials and experiences from both a learning and practical experience perspective. Adding a professional coach to your project team can do miracles for your discipline of execution. Coaches remove bottlenecks, address particular points of resistance, infiltrate the C-suite, deliver tough messages, deploy communication tactics, and so on. There's a cost to coaching but the payback is real provided that you do proper vetting.

6. Distribute knowledge about execution discipline

If you know your organization lacks a discipline of execution, begin training key players in your pricing project on execution and accountability. That will need to be included in your training roadmap, and you might have to hire specialized consultants for it. There are good books focusing on execution (see *Execution: The Discipline of Getting Things Done* by Larry Bossidy and Ram Charan, 2002; and *The 4 Disciplines of Execution [4DX]: Achieving Your Wildly Important Goals* by Chris McChesney, Sean Covey, and Jim Huling, 2016) as well as videos on YouTube. Make sure to include a module on execution in your training content. You can create the content yourself by finding readily available videos, papers, and books. This is the minimum you should think of doing if you're on your own and you're facing an uphill battle in pricing execution.

7. Launch a 4DX initiative for your project

Ask your strategy office or PMO whether 4DX is currently being used or is being introduced to the organization. Franklin Covey defines 4DX as a process to teach leaders how to help their teams execute on their highest priorities amid the whirlwind of the day to day. Specifically, Covey proposes four important dimensions:

- Focus on the wildly important
- Act on the lead measures
- Keep a compelling scoreboard
- Create a cadence of accountability

Many organizations have applied the 4DX process, but it might not have reached the pricing office yet. It's worth finding out whether the process has been deployed to quickly integrate some of the principles into your pricing projects. If it isn't currently adopted in your organization, nothing stops you from using the process to boost the execution intensity in your pricing project. A first step could be for you to get certified in the 4DX process. See www.franklincovey.com for more information.

8. Allocate budget for execution

You're in charge of your pricing strategy, your pricing initiatives and your pricing execution plan. It is therefore up to you to reinforce the focus on execution. You have to be accountable, and you should never be blamed for introducing specific change management and execution programs in your planning and budgeting. You owe it to yourself to maximize your chances of execution success. Ultimately, your budget and plans might be cut. Your execution programs might be eliminated, and you might be asked to do more of that work yourself. This is when you need the courage to push back and ask for a minimum investment to focus on execution. The first step is to include execution budgets in your plans. The second is to push back and to make sure you get some support. The last step is for you to decide whether you can do the specific project without a change management and execution focus. That's a philosophical question for another day!

If you're working for a large organization, you might have access to some of the corporate resources such as project managers, change managers, execution training, or internal coaches. If you're not, it's obviously a bit more constraining. You might have to become the project and change manager yourself. That means getting trained and certified in the disciplines and using the tools in your pricing program. The bottom line is that you need to build your own toolbox to improve your probability of execution success. Remember that 70 percent of change projects typically fail. That's a high number, and you want to maximize your chances of being in the 30 percent that succeeds. In pricing, 50 percent of the impact comes from strategies and 50 percent comes from execution. You can't ignore half the pie.

Index

Page numbers in *italics* refer to figures

5C model 19–20
8-step change model 11–12; Bayer AG 92–3

ability to pay (ATP) 139
"absorptive capacity" 90
account managers: role of 45–6
account pricing plan 47–8
Adobe: digital transformation of 3–4
Agility: digital business agility 4
AI (artificial intelligence): identifying opportunities and risks 155–6
allocating budgets for execution 161–2
Amazon 37
analytics: Disney Company 24–32
Anderson, James 127, 137
approach to mastering bidding challenges: Pricing to Win 111–20
artificial intelligence (AI): identifying opportunities and risks 155–6
assigning value and measure: Pricing to Win 115–16
ATP (ability to pay) 139
automation: identifying opportunities and risks 155–6

B2B (business-to-business) 78; designing segmentation 80–2; offer dispersion 103; pricing 103–4; quantifying value proposition *132*; segmentation 78–80; value propositions 114; value quantification 104–7, 122–3
B2B purchase criteria: mapping 107–9
B2C (business-to-consumer): segmentation 78
best practices: for designing customer segmentation 81–2; pricing execution 159–62; pricing strategies 157–8; for training programs for price execution 91
best-in-class companies 39–40, 74
biases 32
bid positioning: Pricing to Win 116–20
bidding challenges: Pricing to Win 111–20

budgets: customer budgets 114; for pricing execution 161–2
business culture: quantified value propositions 139
buyers 38
buy-in: Disney Company 25–8, 30–1
buying process: value proposition 144–5

CAP (Change Acceleration Process) 12–14
capabilities of: sales managers 72
car buying process 38
Cespedes, Frank: interview with 37–44
change management 160; value quantification 131
change management considerations 60
change management indicators 159
changes in sales force compensation 57–8
changing sales force compensation 59–60, 63–5
changing purchasing criteria of purchasers 75–6
characteristics of: sales managers 41–3, 75; SAMs (strategic account managers) 51–2
coaches: value and pricing coaches 160–1
collaboration: value quantification 130
commercial excellence programs: interview with Bernard Quancard 45–54
compensation: sales force compensation 56–65
competition: Pricing to Win 115
consolidating pricing-related information 152–3
controlling prices: steps to 152–8
cost-based pricing 43–4
co-value creation 47, 49, 53–4
customer budgets: Pricing to Win 114
customer culture: quantified value propositions 139
customer insight: value quantification 124–5
customer orientation: value quantification 129–31
customer purchase criteria: mapping B2B purchase criteria 107–9
customer segmentation 78; B2B (business-to-business) 78–80; data 79–80; designing 80–2; executing through scientific selling 84; guidelines for execution 85–6; operationalizing 82–5

customer selection 130
customer-centric selling: value propositions 149–50

dashboard of procurement: SAMs (strategic account managers) 52–3
dashboards: pricing execution 160
data: Pricing to Win 115–16; sales force compensation 62–3; segmentation 79–80
data biases 32
DDAC (Disney Data and Analytics Conference) 24–5
designing segmentation 80–2
DHL 51–2
differentiation: value quantification 125–6
digital business agility 4
digital transformation of Adobe 3–4
"direct the rider": switch model 14
discipline of execution 161
discounting practices: interview with Jose Vela 71–7
Disney Company: interview with Mark Shafer 22–32
Disney Data and Analytics Conference (DDAC) 24–5
Documented Solutions for SKF 137
documenting value quantification 129–31

EBIT (earnings before interest and taxes) 103–4
ecosystem captains: SAMs (strategic account managers) 46
effective discounting practices: interview with Jose Vela 71–7
ethnographic research 125
Evangalytics 24–5, 30, 32
examples of quantified value propositions 131–3
excellence in pricing strategy implementation 40–1
executing: customer segmentation 83–4; guidelines for segmentation 85–6
execution discipline 161

financial and pricing indicators 159
flexibility: training programs for pricing execution 88–9
forecasting: Disney Company 27
frameworks for pricing strategy implementation: 5C model 19–20; 8-step change model 11–12; Change Acceleration Process (CAP) 12–14; free spaces theory 17–19; McKinsey influence model 15–17; switch model 14–15; transformation triangle 17
free spaces theory 17–19
"freemium" 39–40

General Electric: Change Acceleration Process (CAP) 12–14
guidelines for executing segmentation 85–6

high-quality value model 142
Hinterhuber & Partners 109, 132
hybrid segmentation process *83*
hybrid value agreement 140

identifying opportunities and risks with AI and automation 155–6
implementing value quantification 129–31
incentives: sales force compensation 38, 56
innovation: outcome-driven innovation 125
interviews: with Cespedes, Frank 37–44; with Quancard, Bernard 45–54; with Shafer, Mark 22–32; with Vela, Jose 71–7

Jobs, Steve 125

Kellogg, K. C. 17, 19
Kemps, Pascal 46, 51–2
Kotter, J. P. 11
KPI (key performance indicators): defining for pricing execution 159–60; sales force compensation for variable baskets 59

large deals: offer dispersion 103; pricing 103–4, 109; value quantification 104–7
levers 117–18; price *152*
limitations of sales force compensation research 65
Lion King 23
Liozu, S. 19
listening: customer insight 124

machine learning: Disney Company 27–8
mapping: B2B purchase criteria 107–9
margin drivers: tracking 76
marketing planning process *82*
marketing professionals: reasons value-selling initiatives fail 143
marketing strategies: optimizing 84–5
maturity model for pricing guidance *156*
maximum principle 117
McKinsey influence model 15–17
measuring: SAMs (strategic account managers) 50
misalignment of organizational incentives 56
Monitor Group 140
"motivate the elephant": switch model 14–15

Netflix 78

offer dispersion: B2B (business-to-business) 103
operationalizing customer segmentation 82–5
opportunistic customers 76
optimizing marketing strategies 84–5
organizing price information 153–5
outcome-driven innovation 125

PBAs (performance-based agreements) 140
PMOs (project management offices): pricing execution 160
PMPs (project management professionals) 160
pocket-price-brand analysis 75
positioning in a sweet spot: Pricing to Win 118–20
price: co-value creation 47; levers *152*
price controls 151–8
price premium 107
price testing 44
price waterfalls 153–4
pricing 109; profit drivers 103–4; SAMs (strategic account managers) 47–8
pricing authority 38–9; sales managers 72–4
pricing decisions: discussing 155
"pricing evangelist" 71
pricing execution: best practices 159–62; implications for 158; sales force compensation 58–62; training programs for 87–91
pricing guidance maturity model *156*
pricing process: value quantification 140
pricing systems 157
Pricing to Win 111; mastering bidding challenge 111–20
process of value quantification 124–31
procurement: SAMs (strategic account managers) 52–3
product management: reasons value-selling initiatives fail 143
profit drivers: pricing 103–4
project management offices (PMOs): pricing execution 160
purchasers: changing purchasing criteria of purchasers 76

qualitative segmentation 80; best practices 81–2
Quancard, Bernard 107; interview with 45–54
quantified value propositions 136–7; business culture 139; customer culture 139; examples 131–3; value conceptualization 138–9; value quantification 139–41
quantifying value 128–9; large deals 104–7
quantitative segmentation 80

reasons value-selling initiatives fail 143
references: value quantification 131
research: ethnographic research 125; for sales force compensation 56–63
return on investment (ROI) 128
revenue management: interview with Mark Shafer 22–32
rewarding SAMs (strategic account managers) 51
road maps: training programs for pricing execution 88

sales control systems 43
sales force compensation: changing 63–5; research 56–63

sales force environment 43
sales forces: interview with Frank Cespedes 37–44
sales function 122
sales management: reasons value-selling initiatives fail 143
sales managers 49; capabilities of 72; characteristics of 41–3, 75; pricing authority 72–4
SAMA (Strategic Account Management Association) 45
SAMs (strategic account managers) 37–8, 49–50; characteristics of 51–2; measuring 50; pricing 47–8; procurement 52–3; rewarding 51; role of 45–6
SAP: quantified value propositions 133
Schneider Electric 12, 47, 50
segmentation 78; B2B (business-to-business) 78–80; data 79–80; designing 80–2; executing through scientific selling 84; guidelines for execution 85–6; operationalizing 82–5
selling effectiveness 43
Shafer, Mark: interview with 22–32
"shape the path": switch model 14–15
SKF 128–9, 136–7
Spandex Group 71
stakeholders: Pricing to Win 112–14
Strategic Account Management Association (SAMA) 45
strategic account managers (SAMs) 37–8, 49–50; characteristics of 51–2; measuring 50; pricing 47–8; procurement 52–3; rewarding 51; role of 45–6
strategic bid positioning: Pricing to Win 116–20
strategic contextualization 61
strategic levers 117–18
success for value selling 148–9
sweet spots: Pricing to Win 118–20
switch model 14–15
system biases 32

TCO (total cost of ownership) 141
testing prices 44
tracking margin drivers *76*
training programs for pricing execution 87–91
transformation triangle 17
transition time: sales force compensation 60

value 30, 40–1; assigning for Pricing to Win 115–16; co-value creation 47; customer demand for Pricing to Win 113–14
value and pricing coaches 160–1
value-based pricing strategies 140–1
value co-creation 47, 49, 53–4
value conceptualization 138–9
value creation 125–7
value models 142
value proposition experience *148*

value proposition score *147*
value propositions: for customer-centric selling 149–50; value quantification 127–8; value selling 144–5
value quantification 49, 122–3, 128–9, 136–7, 139–41; effective propositions 131–3; large deals 104–7; process of 124–31
Value Quantification Tool 106
value selling 142–3; map for success 148–9; reasons for failure 143; sales and marketing alignment 144–5; value propositions for customer-centric selling 149–50
value-based incentives 56
value-based selling 140

value-price relationships: Pricing to Win 116
value-selling initiatives: accelerating 145–8
value-selling success *138*
variable basket: pricing KPI (key performance indicator) 59; sales force compensation 63
Vela, Jose: interview 71–7
vice president of value 137

Walt Disney Company: interview with Mark Shafer 22–32
Welch, Jack 12–14
WTP (willingness to pay) 139

Zurich 48, 51